D0350306

AN ALMOST PERFECT CHRISTMAS

AN
ALMOST
PERFECT
CHRISTMAS

NINA STIBBE

Little, Brown and Company
New York   Boston   London

Copyright © 2017 by Nina Stibbe
Illustrations © 2017 by Lauren Tamaki

Little, Brown and Company
Hachette Book Group
1290 Avenue of the Americas, New York, NY 10104
littlebrown.com

First United States Edition: November 2018
Originally published in Great Britain by Viking, November 2017

Little, Brown and Company is a division of Hachette Book Group, Inc. The Little, Brown name and logo are trademarks of Hachette Book Group, Inc.

The publisher is not responsible for websites (or their content) that are not owned by the publisher.

The following pieces appeared in different form in the following publications. The author would like to gratefully acknowledge permission to reproduce them in this book: 'Turkey and Me' and 'How to Win the Battle of Christmas as a Guest—or as a Host' in *The Guardian;* 'Going Home for Christmas' in *Psychologies;* 'Christmas Shopping' in *Sainsbury's Magazine;* 'The Christmas Lunch: A Story' in *The Spectator;* and 'Timothy the Christmas Turkey: A Story' in *The Stylist.*

The Hachette Speakers Bureau provides a wide range of authors for speaking events. To find out more, go to hachettespeakersbureau.com or call (866) 376-6591.

ISBN 978-0-316-41581-1
LCCN 2018944946

10 9 8 7 6 5 4 3 2 1

LSC-C

Printed in the United States of America

For Kate Nunney – upholder of Christmas tradition

CONTENTS

AN ALMOST PERFECT CHRISTMAS

TURKEY AND ME

I vowed from a young age to never cook a turkey, and I never have – unless you count turkey mince (which I don't). I mentioned this early on to my partner, along with other possible deal-breakers – such as my laziness, love of dogs, and plan to have six children – and he seemed fine with it all.

Later, when I was pregnant with the first of the six children, I told him that – parent-wise – I was planning to model myself on Jill Archer, fictional matriarch from *The Archers* – who I'd have chosen as my own mother, if you could choose. I must've inadvertently mentioned this to my actual mother because ever since then she hasn't missed an opportunity to say how awful Jill Archer is, and how badly she compares to other mothers such as Joan Crawford or Wilma Flintstone.

Some months later, one evening at the very end of

October 1999, I was half listening to a tiny transistor radio when I heard Jill Archer saying to her younger fictional daughter, 'It's only eight weeks away, darling, you need to order your Christmas turkey as soon as possible.'

'Did you hear that?' I hissed, grabbing my partner by the sleeve. 'Jill Archer just said it's only eight weeks until Christmas.'

And I reminded him that if he wanted a turkey he'd have to buy it and cook it himself and not involve me in any way or make heavy weather of it.

I was in a maternity hospital bed at the time, surrounded by women trying to get their brand-new babies to latch on. I stopped liking fictional matriarch Jill Archer (briefly). I felt anxiety rising inside, and my partner could sense it too. The whole ward could sense it – all the brand-new babies began to cry, and those that had latched on, latched off. My own baby daughter – who hadn't, according to the midwife, ever *officially* latched on – bawled and began to hate me.

'We don't *have* to have turkey,' said my partner, 'let's just chill with a chop.' And because 'chill with a chop' was a really hip thing to say in 1999 – and all the women in the beds around me could probably feel Christmas looming, too – a quiet little cheer went up (quiet because of the babies, but loud in spirit). A competitive male at a neighbouring bed said he'd do chops, too, and then another said they might have ready-made beef Wellingtons from Waitrose. And soon not a single one of them was going to be having turkey, and a great sense of well-being descended on the ward.

Years later, my turkey-cooking phobia remains and we've had chops every year since – except for the year we had Dairylea sandwiches. Why am I so turkey-phobic, you might wonder. Well, it's because I've seen the damage turkeys can do and the tyrannical hold they have over otherwise robust, rational people and I've 'been affected'. It goes back to childhood.

My mother is not a foodie. She hates all foods and would even hate that I've written 'foods' like that – with an 's'. She would prefer that all meals be taken in pill form and avoids cooking at all costs and, as far as I can tell, she only eats peanuts, raw carrots and the occasional plum. But once a year, every year, she becomes possessed of a deep and profound need to serve up a roast turkey. It's some kind of grim personal quest.

After leaving her children to survive from day to day on sugar sandwiches, and toast and Blue Band, suddenly at Christmas the turkey would appear and our mother would almost kill herself in the kitchen, trying to please it; to provide the trimmings and keep it moist, only for it to roast itself dry and then be gone from our lives for the next twelve months.

She's not alone – many are afflicted in this way – only, in my mother's case, it seems so unfair, her being not only food-shy but a rebel and a free spirit in everything else.

For as long as I can remember, the idea of Christmas dinner would pop into her head in early autumn, when she was supposed to put in a Christmas meats order at the local butcher. Not fully knowing who might be with us and requiring turkey on the day, and faced with a walk into the village, though, she might think 'Oh, fuck it' and just get one at Sainsbury's on December 23rd with the main shop. Then, on December 23rd, not wanting a fist fight over a fresh one in the supermarket, she might opt for a frozen one from Bejam (or later, Iceland) and leave it to defrost in the downstairs toilet for not quite forty-eight hours.

Before dawn on the 25th – this was when resentment might begin to creep in – before stockings had been opened, one of my siblings or me might be dragged out of bed and forced to sit cross-legged on the toilet floor pointing a Philips hairdryer on an extension lead into the chest cavity for half an hour to finish off the defrosting.

Still in the early hours of Christmas Day – the bird more or less thawed – the cooking preparation would begin. The methods have varied over the years, all with a view to combating dryness. Moistness being the main objective and coming only slightly behind non-toxicity and hugeness.

It goes without saying that all manner of liquids were tried out in the baking tray and various fatty meats laid over the breast. And, oven-temp-wise, my mother has tried the high-then-low, low-then-high, constant-medium and the fast blast. And, timings-wise, the quick, the slow and the very slow. And usually cooked the stuffing separately for a more even finish and crispy topping – and to prevent it pre-venting the bird cooking through.

For a while, influenced by something she'd read in the *Observer*, she'd turn the bird breast-side down. The unstable position making mid-cook basting quite perilous. The result ('quite dry') was not helped by its wonky, pale and unappetizing appearance. Around 1981 she started covering the (now) upturned breast with a butter-impregnated muslin cloth (or J Cloth), as recommended by her friend Lynn Horse-pole – who ran a catering company and claimed to produce drippingly moist turkeys all through the year, albeit for pies and coronation turkey (a wedding staple). Lynn was a keen disciple of Fanny Cradock but never used the 'F' word in front of my mother because of her reputation for rebelling dramatically against shouty dictators like Fanny.

In spite of continued dryness, my mother stuck with Lynn's (Fanny) method until the year she heard about

Delia's 'loose foil wrap' (everyone was talking about it, even Lynn Horsepole) and she very much took to Delia's sympathetic, non-combative style ('What's ten or twenty minutes between friends on Christmas Day?') and, although she enjoyed some psychological progress, in truth, the turkey was still dry.

A few years later, she copied the protagonist in an American novel (Anne Tyler?) and tried injecting a mix of butter and olive oil under the skin. This method required some medical training and hourly basting from 4 a.m. The turkey baster itself turned up a few times for various plot reasons (in the novel) but in real life the result was still 'on the dry side'.

More recently still, she has followed Lynn Horsepole into a 'cider bath' – based on Nigella's seasoned brining method. Everyone rejoiced at this because we all love and want to emulate Nigella whenever possible – but it required the central heating to be turned down unacceptably low for the twenty-four hours of the brining and she and my stepfather got cold feet (literally) and she went back to Delia's steamy foil, which had given the best result (though still 'dry-ish').

One year, not that long ago, but before Delia, an American neighbour, Mrs Wolfe, told my mother, 'Americans do not know the meaning of dry turkey,' and insisted – in the American way – that she try her Kentucky-style Butterball turkey fryer, because this was the true secret to turkey moistness. My mother had been on the brink of trying it until another neighbour (a worrier) reminded my mother that Mrs Wolfe had burnt her veranda down with the fryer on Thanksgiving some years before because she hadn't been one hundred per cent vigilant with the hot oils near so much wood. Remembering this, my mother questioned the likelihood of her own vigilance with the hot oils and decided not to risk it — not that she has a veranda to burn down, but there was the shed and some unruly shrubs.

Each year, Christmas lunchtime would begin somewhere between 2 p.m. and 5 p.m. The bird — having been planned, bought, defrosted, prepared, cooked and tended to like a mare about to foal — would be heaved up on to the festive tablecloth and set down next to dishes of mash and sprouts, plus a jug of 'gravy'. The assembled nervous diners would all wait for someone else to comment, and some brave fool would mutter 'delicious' or 'so moist' or something, and my mother would give him or her a withering look, chuck a few peanuts into her mouth and light a cigarette. The party would eat quietly until my plateless mother might pick a tiny piece off the bird and declare it, 'Dry as a bone — as per usual.' Then it'd be over for another year.

I often amuse myself remembering the year my granny took a small forkful of white meat and, after swilling it down with a glass of water, asked, 'Did you baste it?'

I can laugh about the past, but in truth my phobia persists. I know this because, very recently, faced with a Norfolk Bronze turkey crown in the New Forest, I fled the scene and spoke tearfully on the phone to my stepfather from a lay-by.

I may as well explain.

We were spending Christmas at my mother-in-law's house. We'd offered to cook our usual (lamb chops) for eight people, including guests who'd be arriving for a one o'clock Christmas lunch but leaving at four o'clock sharp for a flight. We'd been about to go shopping at the crack of dawn on Christmas Eve, when our host told us that another family member – who *wouldn't* be with us on the day – had already got the shopping in and, although it wasn't what we were expecting (chops), there was lots of it and it was in the freezer (turkey). I let out an involuntary cry and my partner did that thing with his hands – the internationally recognized sign for 'everything's going to be OK' – and said, 'Leave it with me.'

Later that day, at about 5 p.m., when Granny Kate was telling us the individual histories of the assorted owls on her Christmas tree, he interrupted. He wanted the wifi code. He'd forgotten to take the turkey out of the freezer and needed to get online, he said, to find super-quick turkey defrosting methods. I quietly and privately freaked out and drove to Ringwood – a nearby market town with good supermarket representation – chanting as I drove, 'I fucking knew it, I fucking knew it.' Once there, I ran from store to store, begging for any old turkey that wasn't frozen, and I have to say the grocery staff of Ringwood really let themselves down that night.

Leaving the car park in a kind of daze, I took the wrong exit off a mini roundabout and soon found myself on the outskirts of Bournemouth. I pulled into a lay-by. I was distraught, lost, miles away from home, and a couple in the Skoda Yeti parked in front of me seemed to be naked. I tried to gather my thoughts. Should we risk poisoning my dear mother-in-law, the soon-to-fly-abroad guests, an immunocompromised relative, my own dear little children, my partner and myself with a toxic bacon-lattice-topped, extra-large turkey crown? Or admit defeat and serve up parsnip and cranberry omelette (I'd bought a dozen eggs in Waitrose)? I rang my mother. She congratulated me on the dozen eggs, commiserated about the turkey and put me on to my stepfather, and he talked sense.

'There's nothing more you can do now, love. Leave it to Mark, it's not the end of the world, just follow the A31 to Ringwood and get yourself back to the house.'

I heard my mother heckling in the background.

'What's she saying?' I asked.

11

'She says get the radio on, it's *The Archers*, and you might get some turkey advice from your beloved Jill.'

We laughed.

'OK,' I said, 'and by the time I get back, all will be well in Ambridge and the world.'

Back at the house, the tree was still twinkling in the window and the hundred owls peeped out from its branches. No one had even noticed I'd been gone. My partner was up to his elbows – performing the water defrosting method – and the turkey was well on the way to being sufficiently thawed for tomorrow's lunch. You can look this method up (it does actually work, but the water must be cold, never warm).

I went through to the lounge where the others were watching the end credits of *Sinkhole Tragedies* on the True-Life Emergency Channel (my mother-in-law's favourite).

My daughter looked up. 'Have you been crying?'

'I was listening to *The Archers*,' I said.

'Oh, was Jill Archer being poignant and Christmassy?'

'No, it was Lynda Snell's lost dog, Scruff – he's safe and well,' I said.

'I don't know what you're on about,' she said.

My partner called through from the turkey defrosting bay, 'What's happened?'

'Lynda heard noises at the back door, and it was Scruff – he's home!' I called back.

'No, I meant the sinkhole,' he called back. 'Did they get the bloke out?'

'No,' called my mother-in-law, 'they couldn't risk it.'

I texted my mother: 'Jill Archer no help, but turkey is melting ok anyway, lolz. But OMG, Scruff!'

And she replied: 'Jill Archer = fkn useless. Yes, so happy abt Scruff – hurrah!'

And I settled down to watch *When Birds Attack*.

You'll be relieved to know that the turkey was fully defrosted by the early hours of Christmas Day and my partner served it up at 1 p.m. on the dot. Everyone said it was perfect and moist – and it actually was (albeit no bread sauce, only cranberry) – and no one got even slightly ill or died.

Postscript: In the early autumn of this year, my sister called with turkey news.

My mother has ordered a high-welfare bird *online*. It'll be delivered to her door, in a refrigerated vehicle, ready basted and loose-foiled. She plans to cook it on Christmas Eve (an old Keith Floyd idea) and will slice and heat it on Christmas Day in a dish of wine-rich gravy on the bottom shelf of the oven.

It's failsafe, apparently.

'Good luck to her,' I said.

'You could give it a try, too,' said my sister, 'and stop having those awful chops that everyone hates.'

SWIM TO SANTA CLAUS: A Story

ecause it was just Jeanne and me, things were quite intense, especially at Christmas. Jeanne was my mother but I was in the habit of calling her Jeanne (pronounced the French way with a soft 'J' – 'Sha'). I have few memories of my father (I'd have called him Henrik if I'd known him longer) because he and Jeanne separated when I was a small child and he went off somewhere far away, like Lapland.

My main memory of Henrik was when he was doing seasonal work at Fenwick's of Leicester and he was given the job of digging the Christmas grotto out of the storeroom and assembling it.

'It's a bit bleak,' he told us. 'If I were Santa Claus, I'd want it cosy.'

And with a few pieces of wood and some split logs Henrik made a lifelike, two-dimensional fireplace for the grotto and took it into work, where he added some red foil flames that appeared to dance upon the logs. Everyone, including Father Christmas himself, admired it and Henrik was invited to take full charge of the grotto, and he made it very beautiful indeed.

One night in early December, Henrik came home and told us that Father Christmas — an ex-warehouseman — had suddenly died. A whole lot of staff who'd been with Fenwick's longer than Henrik, including the white-bearded husband of the head of scarves, had scrabbled (distastefully) for the position, which was, barring accidents, ninety-nine per cent sitting down. But because of the beautiful work he'd done on the grotto – and in spite of his accent – Henrik had been given it. This was a lot to take in for me at such a tiny age. I went to bed that night knowing that Father Christmas was dead, that Henrik would be taking over, and for some reason (I couldn't quite fathom) Jeanne found the whole thing hysterical.

One day soon afterwards, Jeanne took me to Fenwick's to see Father Christmas — officially — even though she and Henrik had agreed it might be best not to. We queued like ordinary customers and, not knowing what to expect, I felt anxious. Once we'd caught sight of Henrik in the costume, Jeanne became hysterical again and had to stifle snorts of laughter and dab mirthful tears from her eyes with a little handkerchief.

When my turn came, she pulled herself together. 'Remember, he's Father Christmas,' she whispered, '*not* Daddy!'

Seeing me, Henrik turned and made a desperate gesture to Jeanne. But Jeanne just plonked me in his lap and took a photograph – a blurry one, as it turned out. Henrik pretended not to know me, and asked simple questions that a real father should know, such as, 'What's your name?' and, 'What are you hoping to get for Christmas?'

I stayed silent. I couldn't work out who the joke was on – or who we were keeping the secret from – and after a few uncomfortable moments Jeanne dragged me away.

She was cross. 'You've lost your chance now,' she said.

I looked back as another kid climbed on to Henrik's knee. I'd lost my chance.

'It was disrespectful of you to have brought her, Jeanne. I asked you not to,' said Henrik, at home later, 'it was awkward.'

'You're damned right it was awkward,' said Jeanne, 'the pair of you clamming up like we were committing some kind of crime. Jesus!'

Not long after that, Henrik threw our Christmas tree away with the rubbish sooner than Jeanne would have liked, and she lost her rag. I think it was a 'last straw' for Jeanne, or maybe for Henrik, and it was the last time I ever saw him.

After that, I could never quite clear a muddle in my mind, and if I'm honest, I sometimes got quite het up in Christmas grottos.

One time, I believed so strongly that Father Christmas was Henrik that I threw my arms around him, gripped the fabric of his cloak in my fists and buried my face in his armpit. Jeanne had taken a photograph before realizing the situation had turned weird. I have that picture still – me, clinging like a baby koala, and him, spectacles and beard askew. Jeanne pulled at my sleeve and tried to prise my fingers open – but only having two hands, and being in high heels, she struggled and I found her easy to resist.

I clung on.

'Help me out here!' she hissed at Father Christmas, but he'd been trained to sit it out for legal reasons.

I remember peeping through my screwed-up eyelids at the astonished children waiting in the line. 'It's my dad,' I shouted to them.

Eventually, Jeanne asked him to lower his beard to prove he was no relation. He wouldn't do that either, it being against the rules – except in an emergency.

Jeanne suggested he move further into the grotto — for privacy — and then lower it. He refused and, in the end, Jeanne lunged at him, grabbed it and tugged it off. Father Christmas cried out in great pain, fell backwards off his little chair and held his ears. I could see straight away then, he wasn't Henrik. Several customers demanded their money back and a woman appeared with a first-aid kit.

The following year, we went again to Fenwick's — incognito. I was high on a mixture of excitement and dread. Jeanne could sense it and, when our turn came, she asked Father Christmas if he wouldn't mind lowering the beard a tiny bit.

'Just so she can see who you are.'

He did, and I saw it was Henrik.

'Henrik!' I shouted and fell on him.

'It's not Henrik, baby,' said Jeanne. 'It's not him.'

'It is,' I sobbed, and clung.

'It isn't,' said Jeanne, 'let go of him.'

'It is Henrik,' I cried.

'I'm not Henry,' he said.

'Hen*rik*,' I corrected.

A strong member of staff escorted us out of the building, and I cried for two days — because it *was* Henrik.

I was forbidden to see Father Christmas after that. Forbidden by Jeanne and banned from Fenwick's.

I didn't let it stop me, though. I snuck into various grottos I came across. You wouldn't believe how many

Santas were around, back then, and people were crazy for them. I saw funny old ones in church rooms; chubby, authentic ones in toyshops; thin, ropy-looking ones in village halls. I saw a glorious, realistic one at Glebe Garden Centre where, if you bought a sprig of Christmas foliage, you got to see him for free, in a Christmas glade. And, one time, at the Pork Pie Library, where, if you were a member (I was), you could hear him read a poem of your choice. I chose a Spike Milligan, which went down a storm. The child after me chose a Robert Frost, and he said he'd read that out four times already that day.

It all came to an end around my thirteenth birthday, in early December. Jeanne and I had a tearful talk. Jeanne said that we both needed to move on from unhelpful behaviours. By which she meant my visits to Father Christmas – she guessed I was sneaking off to see him on account of all the pointless little items and oranges that she kept finding. He'd started doing after-school sessions in Freeman's toyshop and by the time of our talk, I'd already seen him twice there and once at a junior school Christmas Fayre.

This Christmas would mark the eight-year anniversary of her split with Henrik, she told me, and if she'd known she'd still be single when I hit the teen years, she said, she'd never have chucked him out for chucking the tree out. She'd imagined there'd be 'plenty more fish in the sea' – like the saying – but

there hadn't been. Or if there were, they needed fish-
ing out more forcefully. She was now going to take
her therapist's advice and explore new waters. She
was going to be proactive. And because she needed
my help and full support, she said, it was time for my
childhood to come to an end.

'In what way?' I wondered.

'You've got to grow right up,' she said, 'and gener-
ally be less weird.'

Somehow, the talk ended with my swearing on my
own deathbed that I'd stop visiting Santa – and never
go again until I had my own little child to take – and
Jeanne announcing, in that case, we could get a dog.
Which I'd been mithering for. So we got Megan, a
Labrador cross who'd been well trained but had been
given to the dogs' home because she'd started barking
at people in hats. She was perfect for us (dog novices
who hardly ever wore hats).

The only downside of having Megan was that she
was the living, breathing reminder of the tearful talk
and Jeanne saying what a freak I was, and me admit-
ting it but being too polite to say what a freak *she*
was.

Still, it was very nice having a dog.

Soon Jeanne's deep-sea explorations resulted in an
affair with a podgy philosopher from the university
called Mike Melrise. They'd met at a seminar about

existence and they'd ended up having sex afterwards in a lecture hall. Even though he wasn't half as nice looking as Henrik (and was married and preferred classical to pop), he'd had a paper published about how the sex in the novels of D. H. Lawrence had affected the female psyche in the second half of the twentieth century, and a whole book on literary sex in general – and this forensic knowledge of fictional sex was a powerful aphrodisiac, according to Jeanne.

Although they had agreed to keep it 'clean', Jeanne had started to break the rules. Not because she'd fallen in love with him but because she became interested in his life – like when you start a jigsaw puzzle and need to have the pieces all spread out in front of you, to see where you are. She didn't just do the ordinary proactive things – like looking up his address in the phone book and following him to his office on the university campus – she also followed his wife to Woolco and the hairdresser. And she kept tabs on his daily movements via the academic diary he kept in his car. She didn't do this in a sneaky, immoral kind of way, but just to ascertain whether he'd be thinking about Hegel or Plato (or D. H. Lawrence) and she might therefore know his frame of mind and whether he'd be dining in or out, or going to see a play and so forth. And this diary spying was how she noticed that Mike and his wife and children would be attending the Santa Claus Swim Party at the municipal pool on the Saturday before Christmas. And why, on the morning of that day, Jeanne told me to get my swimming kit ready and shave my legs because I looked like a gorilla from the knee down.

'But I'm banned from seeing Father Christmas,' I said. 'I've just promised you I'll never go to see him again.'

'We're not going to *see* Father Christmas – as such,' said Jeanne. 'Primarily, we're going to watch Mike's family interact and, in particular, see his wife's bikini.'

'Why?' I asked.

'A bikini can tell you a lot,' she said.

I didn't want to shave my legs for the first time under these circumstances, so Jeanne did it for me in the back garden. I closed my eyes and, although it was a strange sensation, I was relieved at how quick and painless it was.

'For a better result,' she said, 'do it with soapsuds, in the bath.'

'But are we invited?' I asked, as we sped along the lanes towards the town pool.

'You don't have to be invited to a public event at the municipal pool,' said Jeanne, 'it's for everyone.'

She explained that she wanted to assess the situation between Mike and his wife and, if possible, show herself in a good enough light that Mike might theoretically consider switching from situation A (living with his wife and children) to situation B (living with Jeanne and me).

'We have to seem to offer something he doesn't currently have but would quite like,' said Jeanne.

We arrived.

Mike's maroon Renault with its distinctive registration was parked right by the door and underneath the banner strung across the entrance: *Today – Swim to Santa Claus – under 10s.*

'Only under tens can swim to Santa's pontoon for the gift and medal,' said the woman on the desk, looking at me.

'She loves Santa,' Jeanne told the woman, 'she's just one of those big, simple kids – and I'm her accompanying adult.'

I hadn't had lunch and the chlorine aroma was making my stomach rumble. I asked Jeanne if we might have an oxtail soup from the vending machine, or a Kit Kat, to keep me going, but Jeanne was keen to get into the water. She was a bag of nerves, to be honest.

In Female Changing we saw Mrs Melrise and the children – Jennifer and Mike Junior – straight away and although, at first, they seemed quite posh – having a special swimming basket containing drying talcum, a packet of crackers and a bottle of squash for afterwards – it turned out that Marianne Melrise was Canadian, that was all. Her bikini was nice. Not sexy like my mother's stringy one, which showed her whole back and was really just four tiny triangles of spotty red-and-white cotton. Marianne Melrise's was a bit higher up and the bra part was rock solid and completely hid her nipples. It was a 1950s style, both old-fashioned and very stylish. Very grown up.

Sloshing through the footbath behind Jennifer Melrise, I found myself looking at her seersucker swimsuit in a critical way and then saw Mike Junior wearing water wings – aged at least seven years of age – yikes, what a baby.

In the pool area Marianne Melrise climbed carefully backwards down the metal steps and then held her arms up for her son. 'Come on, Mikey!' she coaxed. 'Come on, buddy.'

Mikey hesitated and when he finally went, it was the worst jump I'd ever seen. He hit the water backside first with a huge splash that drenched his mother. When he bobbed up, spluttering, I was surprised to see Marianne not livid at him but grinning.

'Wow, super jump!' she lied.

A whole load of impatient children were queuing up along the side of the pool to swim a shallow width over to see Santa on his inflated pontoon. I kept well away, not wanting to annoy Jeanne and break our pact, but a quick glance revealed that he looked nothing like Henrik – too narrow in the shoulders, and a pot belly.

Jeanne appeared – she'd been ages at the mirror, putting her hair into a mermaidy side-pony. Supporting herself lightly on the handrails above the steps, she dipped to trail her foot through the water – testing the temperature – and then dived straight in, cleanly, barely making a ripple. Everyone waited to see her come up and, when she did, she dived right back down again.

I saw Jennifer Melrise preparing to jump, holding her nose and lining her toes up so they just hung over the pool edge, so I dived in – just like Jeanne (don't worry, you were allowed to dive in those days). It wasn't my best ever dive but a damned sight better than Jennifer's over-prepared pencil jump into the shallow end, which she did the moment I surfaced.

The Melrise children were coming over as a bit sissyish – panicking and hanging on to the poolside – and, not counting my belly flop, Jeanne and I must've looked like a pair of young dolphins on the ocean by comparison. I tried to say something clever involving Jeanne's 'fish-in-the-sea' metaphor but over-explained it and Jeanne became agitated and told me to, 'Shut up and do an underwater handstand or something.'

All we needed, I thought, was a baby brother to challenge little Mikey to a width race and probably do the whole width underwater and come up beaming – unlike little Mikey who, I noticed, was barely keeping it together, gulping like a fish and not pushing his hair out of his eyes, so that his mother had to keep doing it for him. I couldn't decide whether he was a professional attention-seeker or just plain terrified. Either way, what father would want a kid like that?

I swam width after width – some underwater, some breaststroke and a few backstroke. The thing was, though: Mike was nowhere to be seen. After swimming about a mile of assorted styles, I butterflied out to Jeanne who was floating around the six-foot marker, looking cool with her ten candy toenails showing just above the water, like an arty postcard.

Jeanne was thinking the exact same thing as me. 'Where the hell is Mike?' she said.

I doggy-paddled a complete circle, like a seal, and shrugged. There really was no sign of him. Jeanne trod water, miraculously, with her upper body still and high out of the water. And though her legs were going ten to the dozen underneath, she looked rather statuesque – in the classical, decorative sense, not the tall sense. She seemed nonchalant. Nonchalance was definitely her look, even in a municipal pool; it was a thing she'd perfected over the years. It was slightly compromised by the fact that she was gazing so hard at the entrance to Male Changing, it spoiled the look. She should have been looking out of the huge window – out towards the drum factory. That's where I'd have looked, but Jeanne wasn't in possession of her usual self-control. It was Christmas and she was addled by that advice from her stupid therapist, that was why.

I have to say that Mike Melrise's wife, Marianne, seemed nice. It should have been her staring at the Male Changing – she had more right than Jeanne, seeing as Mike should have been out there helping with those two demanding children. But she was just quietly being ever so patient – reassuring and encouraging them and pretending they were good swimmers. She caught my eye, smiled and cocked her head as if she slightly recognized me. I smiled back. Her bikini *was* nice. Jeanne, on the other hand, was now flagging and her bikini was like soggy dish-rags. I wondered if she felt as I did – that Marianne Melrise would be hard to beat, as a wife.

Looking at Jeanne, I realized I was very hungry. My fingers were ridged and waterlogged, and I was beginning to worry about Megan, who was waiting in the car. I climbed out on to the poolside and looked out of the window. Megan seemed fine. She was licking the windows.

Jeanne appeared beneath me and gestured with her eyes to the other side of the pool, where Jennifer was holding the side and doing silly frog kicks. 'Go and ask the daughter where Mike is,' said Jeanne.

I swam over to Jennifer and started doing frog kicks beside her.

'Is that your mother?' I asked, pointing to Marianne.

'Yes,' said Jennifer, 'is that yours – in the dotty bikini?'

'Yes,' I said.

'You don't look alike,' said Jennifer.

She sounded opinionated. *Well*, I thought, *what did I expect from a kid with a sex-obsessed father and a Canadian mother with her own car?*

'Is your dad here?' I asked.

'No,' said Jennifer – defensively, I thought.

'Where is he?' I asked.

'He's not coming to the pool.' She smirked, as if she knew something.

I swam and told Jeanne the bad news. She was disappointed. She swam sloppily over to the poolside, hoisted herself unceremoniously on to the tiles and sat there biting her nails, staring at the Melrises and not even holding her tummy in.

I followed.

'Come on,' she said, eventually, 'let's go get an oxtail soup.'

Sloshing our way through the footbath, Jeanne stopped and grabbed my arm.

'What?' I asked.

'Maybe you *should* swim to Santa.'

She led me back.

'No,' I said, 'I'm too grown up – and I'm forbidden.'

'It's OK,' said Jeanne, 'I *want* you to go.'

This was a turnaround, if ever I'd known one.

But I didn't want to. I didn't believe in that Santa: I could see his horrid little trunks and bare legs. Santa didn't belong in a municipal pool and, in any case, he'd never wear flip-flops. I didn't want to get back into the water, anyway. I was hungry, I was cold, and Megan would be stressing if she didn't see us soon.

'Go on,' said Jeanne, 'go and see Santa one last time.'

I was the last kid in the queue to swim, until Jennifer and Mikey Melrise came and stood behind me.

'Mikey and I will be the last to go,' said Jennifer, as if it was anything to be proud of.

I hugged myself. It wasn't a well-thought-out situation for an encounter with Santa Claus, and not at all Christmassy. Jeanne had positioned herself back on the poolside, up the deep end, and was looking a lot better, propped up on her arms, one leg bent and the other straight, like a model. When it was my turn, I pencil-jumped in and swam the width as quickly as I could. I hadn't the energy to do a proper scoop and pull with my arms, so it was a bit splashy. And by the time

I reached Santa's inflated pontoon, I was exhausted. It took me a couple of attempts to scramble up but Santa greeted me in a most familiar way – by name – and asked how old I was. I said I was nine – but very big for my age. He laughed, as if he was in on the joke.

'Are you here with Jeanne?' he said, pronouncing it perfectly, and I said I was. And he seemed to know a few things about me. He'd seen Megan in the car, he said, and he'd liked Jeanne's dive and that I had a good front crawl and so forth. He knew me. But it wasn't Henrik. I started to feel a bit peculiar – hot and cold at the same time, with a strange rushing feeling in my ears. Santa gave me a gift and a plastic button for swimming the width and signalled for the next child in the line to set off.

My head jerked backwards as I slid off the pontoon and I began to swim away – one-handed – up into the middle of the pool, desperate to tell Jeanne that this funny swimming Santa knew me, and knew her. And if she didn't believe me, she must swim to him herself because he definitely knew us. I definitely wasn't making it up . . .

In the middle of the pool I found my strength had gone. My neck hurt terribly and my toes searched for the bottom of the pool but I was out of my depth. I went under and came up again.

I tried to call out but just took in a mouthful of water. I looked back at Santa and must've done some kind of drowning sign because he stood up out of his inflated shell seat and the whole pontoon wobbled and sent great ripples of water crashing over my head. I thought for a moment he was going to dive in but he didn't.

'Er, can someone help?' he yelled. 'Can someone help that kid?'

I tried to call out to Jeanne but only swallowed another mouthful of water. I tried again and felt myself fading. Water rushed up my nose, and behind my eyes. I flailed, I coughed, I sank, and I bobbed up again, coughed and inhaled yet more water.

Then a jolt and Jeanne was there, holding me, pulling me backwards — one arm under my chin, and the other holding my arms down. I could smell her deodorant — which I thought a miracle. 'OK, baby' she kept saying. 'OK, you just need some oxtail soup, that's all.'

Soon I was on the poolside, wrapped in one of the Melrises' fluffy, tomato-coloured towels. Marianne Melrise was fussing and making sure I was swaddled and talking about double pneumonia. 'Go get the basket, Jen,' she said, 'this little girl needs a shivery bite.'

Everyone was crowding round, applauding Jeanne. Patting her and calling her a hero and a lifesaver and so forth.

Then Santa was there beside Jeanne. He lowered his beard to praise her more clearly, and I saw it was Mike Melrise.

'My *God*,' he said, 'you were marvellous.'

He took off the white trimmed scarlet robe that I loved so much and wrapped it around Jeanne's trembling shoulders and moved a strand of wet hair from her cheek.

'You really *were* marvellous,' Mike said again, '*incredible*.'

I burst into tears of fatigue and joy – and threw up on Mike's flip-flops.

On the way home in the car Megan licked the last little crumbs of powder out of my soup cup and I opened the gift (a token for the vending machine).

Jeanne grinned as she drove.

'Well done, baby,' she laughed, 'but next time you're planning to pull something like that, you got to warn me first, OK.'

'OK,' I said.

HOW TO WIN THE BATTLE OF CHRISTMAS AS A GUEST—OR AS A HOST

Some people think there is no better way to enjoy the festive season than to pack a few winter woollies and throw yourself at the mercy of friends or family. Having spent more than my fair share of Christmases "away" over the years, I have learned that some forward planning is required to maximise the joy. So, let me offer some tried and tested techniques for being the perfect, trouble-free Christmas guest.

1. Food

It is a stressful and chaotic time for your hosts, and that means fallow periods are inevitable – either because the dinner is delayed due to incompetence or oven-timing mixups or because you were seen having muesli and a croissant at breakfast and your host assumes you are not going to need lunch. To avoid headaches, temper tantrums and stomach gripes, you will need emergency snacks.

It is no good hoping snacks will be provided, because they won't. And even if they are available, they will not be easy to find. You can't just ask for a bun or a crumpet, because your hosts will be up to their necks in goose fat and brandy and having a horrible row. You have to be self-sufficient, snack-wise, and arrive with your own stash.

All grown up and alone at last: Christmas away from home is a mixed blessing

Here is what to take: a wedge of cheddar and some Jacob's Cream Crackers, two packs of Warburtons teacakes, a supermarket Yule log and as many Tracker bars as you can fit into your suitcase. Your host might be a bit taken aback when you unload all this, but it is a price worth paying when, less than twenty-four hours later, one of those Warburtons has saved your life.

2. Entertainment

Face it, it is unlikely that you will get to see any decent Christmas telly. All the brilliant stuff that you would have seen had you been allowed to stay at home will be on at the same time as *When Christmas Trees Kill* – your host's favourite – or when someone insists on playing Bait the Weakling (because they do it at that time every year). But you can at least try to seize the agenda.

The first thing to do on arrival at the home of your friend or relative is to announce that it is imperative that you take a shower immediately, then locate the *Radio Times* (it is often down the side of the host's Parker Knoll armchair) and take it into the bathroom with you. Once there, work out your host's marking-up system. (Yellow usually means unmissable. Pink usually means record.) If s/he hasn't flagged your programmes (say, *Call the Midwife*), take out your highlighters and simply do it for them. Replace the magazine and, later on, pick it up and casually mention all the exciting viewing s/he has planned.

It is likely that your host has only three functioning electrical sockets in the whole house. These can therefore become sites of conflict. My advice is to take your own twin-outlet plug adapter with you, plus a mobile charger and some black tape. Bagsy the first empty socket you see, or unplug the Hostess trolley, plug in your adapter and charger and criss-cross with the tape. Charge teenagers' phones and devices for them – in return for their promise not to watch *Mrs Brown's Boys*.

3. Climate

The climate will be your biggest challenge. Your host's home may be too cold. Or it may be too hot. It will certainly not be just right and so you must pack for extreme scenarios. It is no good assuming it will be snuggly inside by the fire, and cold and crisp out-side – that's just on Christmas cards. Take thermals, socks, a good overcoat, and the bizarre tropical outfits you bought for your trip to Sri Lanka. Also a few rolls of bubble wrap.

Don't assume the conditions on a previous visit to this house will prevail. Your relative or friend might have suddenly "gone the other way", either to over-compensate after complaints, or just to mess with you.

It is possible that you will find yourself freezing underneath a flimsy duvet – as at my sister's house, where it is so cold your body partially shuts down. In this case, pop on your thermals and start singing "(Is This the Way to) Amarillo", and do a sort of march-ing exercise. Find an old rug or tarpaulin to throw over your bed, remember the thing about body heat and pompom hats and, if necessary, have the dog in with you, if it is willing.

More likely, and more difficult to survive, is a hot house, in which the central heating is up so high your eyeballs begin dry out – like old roll-on deodorant balls – and it is almost impossible to remain conscious. These conditions call for drastic action.

Do not under any circumstances tell your host you are finding it a bit too hot. Any mention of it will only make matters worse – alerting your host to, and putting paid to, possible tinkering with the thermostat. In fact, the best thing to do is to appear a bit chilly – wear a cardigan and hold your elbows. This will throw the host off the scent. Then, you can open a few windows – but just a crack, so the host doesn't notice. Then, bit by bit, lower the thermostat. But take great care not to be seen. If there are children around, bribe them with sweets to work with you. And, if there are teenagers, bribe them with cigarettes or money. If all fails, appear at tea wearing your swimming costume. And when your hosts object or call the police, tell them you will put your trousers back on if they turn the bloody heating down.

Finally, if at any point you end up leaving in a hurry, remember to take your Warburtons teacakes and cheese with you.

What about the other way around? You are the host. Your casual mention of Christmas in September at a late-summer barbecue has been interpreted as an invitation and some people will be with you from the 24th for three nights.

There is nothing much you can do. Don't be tempted to leak pictures on social media of your house surrounded by masked Rentokil operatives — that isn't fair on the kids. With a bit of careful planning and strict management, your Christmas needn't be entirely ruined.

1. Food

Rule No 1 is to keep your guests well fed and watered. Imagine they are the school hamster and you must do your utmost to keep them at least alive. On the other hand, you don't want it/them to take over your whole lives.

Tea and coffee-making facilities in their bedroom might seem like a faff, but will keep guests at bay in the mornings and stop them bothering you for beverages while they are still in their pyjamas.

Once they have surfaced, usher them to the breakfast buffet and encourage them to really go for it. Include a canister of Swiss-style muesli, assorted bread items and a fan of Kraft cheese slices. This way, they make themselves an emergency cheese roll for later — exactly as if they were at a Holiday Inn — and they might not come bothering you for lunch.

Regarding the festive meal itself, keep expectations low by making jokes about foodie types who make a big fuss about it. And keep appetites low by drip-feeding them snacks such as Quality Street and KP nuts throughout the day. If they try to resist, leave attractive little dishes on the arm of the sofa and retreat. Keep the dog away from them at these times.

Make it quite clear that you would like some help in the kitchen, as they may be too polite to offer. Be aware, though, that this will cause them to march around your kitchen saying, "Have you got a better knife?" or, "Is this your biggest saucepan?" They might even say that, if only they had known how grim your colander was, they would have got you a new one for Christmas. This is all designed to provoke you into releasing them from their task. Don't fall for it. Just say, "I'm sure you'll manage."

2. Entertainment

Like anyone trapped in someone else's home, your guests will be feeling alienated and uncomfortable. Try to alleviate this by leaving a huge, half-finished, 10,000-piece jigsaw puzzle (depicting the sky and sea and a tiny boat) on the dining table. This will become a place of quiet refuge. If your guests finish the puzzle, call the doctor.

Buy two copies of the *Radio Times* and leave a bogus one around for your guests to tamper with. Keep your real marked-up copy in a special hiding place. At any hint that they don't want to watch what you want to watch, tell them that you/your son/your granny has urgent history homework on the subject of, say, 1960s midwifery in the East End of London, and it's absolutely imperative that you/he/she watches the programme in question or it could seriously affect your/his/her chance of a happy, fulfilled life.

If your guests are the type to crave fresh air, avoid having to drive them to local beauty spots by drinking alcohol at the breakfast buffet and throughout the day. Or, tell them you are barred from operating machinery because of the drugs you're taking. Encourage them to walk the dog by doing a long Pilates routine in the lounge.

3. Climate

Keep the house as cold as possible. This might seem wrong and uncosy, but anything warmer than the outside could provoke skimpy clothing and/or lounging around. You need your guests alert for dog-walking and kitchen duties. They may pretend to want it warmer and make jokes about the boiler packing up. Ignore them.

They may suddenly ask to go to church on Christmas Eve or even in the middle of the night. This usually means the house is too hot, they have finished the jigsaw puzzle or they are hoping to buy drugs. If this happens, let them go to church, or if this is complicated or requires a car journey, play them a DVD of *The Vicar of Dibley*, or dig out your copy of *The Ragged Trousered Philanthropists*.

If at any point your guests pack up and leave, make sure they take all their belongings with them and check they haven't accidentally packed your charger.

GOING HOME FOR CHRISTMAS

Until I had children of my own I almost always went home for Christmas to my mother and stepfather's house in Leicestershire – and so did my siblings, all four of them.

We knew that you could only lawfully be excused going home at Christmas if you had:

a) a Christmas-hating spouse and demanding baby twins

b) won a winter-break holiday

c) been sent to prison, or

d) fallen out with everyone.

This meant that, right into our twenties and thirties, there we'd all be, every Christmas – at home.

Many times I tried not to go. I remember one time begging my flatmate, Stella, to stay in London over Christmas and just go to the pub, read Philip Pullman books, write a play or paint our floorboards. She almost agreed but, in the end, decided that the few hellish days at home were an opportunity for her to demonstrate her gratitude to Bob and Jill for bringing her up so nicely – i.e. buying her a flute, explaining the basics of how a democracy works, and teaching her how to grow vegetables. A sort of 'in lieu' payment for all the music lessons and nice soups. Plus, she'd miss seeing Stumpy – the family dog – a needy Jack Russell with itchy skin.

So, I almost always did go home and it should have been awful, and sometimes nearly was.

It used to start in September – around my sister's birthday – when we'd all say to each other, 'Are you going to be at home for Christmas?' and though none of us would want to commit – just in case something more exciting was about to crop up (it did once, for me, but that's another story) – we knew, once we'd had Vic's birthday, Christmas would be upon us in no time at all and, actually, anything cropping up was unlikely.

Then, sometime in late October, my mother would phone round in her special, mardy Christmas voice and ask if we knew yet what our plans were? Because she was about to put in her meats and hams order at the local butcher (a thing she hated almost as much as the cooking bit) and needed to know whether to go for a medium, large or gigantic bird or just a capon and how much sausage meat, etc. At that point you'd have to face up to the fact that you *were* actually going home for Christmas – even though you were twenty-eight years old, or thirty-three – and therefore nothing more exciting had cropped up in your life.

My mother's late-October meat-order enquiry acted as a horrible but useful reminder that our lives were going nowhere. Also, it introduced the idea that there was a bird, somewhere in Norfolk, still at that moment alive and happily pecking corn and bone chippings, unaware that it was about to be ordered for Christmas dinner. So, if you felt a wave of disappointment and regret at that point, you could put it down to sadness about the oblivious turkey.

Then, throughout December, we'd get progress calls, wanting to know when *exactly* (what day, what time) we'd be arriving in Leicestershire and how many meals we might be requiring through the festive period and if any of us had turned vegetarian again. And at that point – not yet having been through the ordeal of Christmas hosting myself (and therefore mistaking essential neurotic *planning* for plain neurotic *hassling*) – I might feel irritated and beleaguered and say I really didn't know.

Sometimes I said things like, 'Relax, Mum, for God's sake, I might not even *be* at home,' just for the hell of it.

Similarly, sometimes my sister might tell my mother she was thinking of bringing her boyfriend with her, even though she knew he wouldn't dream of coming.

And our mother might say, 'That's fine, he's very welcome.'

And then, at the last minute, my sister might say, 'Yeah, well, he couldn't make it.'

And my mother might take it as a snub against her, and then they'd bicker on the phone because my mother had bought a mini torch for his table gift and now it would be wasted.

Before we'd even set off she'd be reminding us not to park on next door's drive, what with it adjoining theirs and being easy to go over the boundary. Especially at Christmas. Nor to make any out-loud comment – or even look at – the OTT Christmas decorations on the Sedgwicks' house across the road (they had CRIMBO in red flashing lights across their porch every year). 'Don't say anything, it encourages them,' she'd say, 'they only do it for attention.'

Christmas Eve would arrive and we'd all be there and the central heating would very much be on and the windows firmly shut. And our old home might seem smaller than it used to, cram-packed with overheated siblings and the odd friend – some smoking, some coughing, some asking to borrow Sellotape – and my asthmatic stepdad using his inhaler. Radio 4 blaring in the kitchen and Radio 2 murmuring in the sitting room. The tree twinkling in its corner – bald already, on account of the terrible dry heat and it having been up since the 5th. And we might look through the Christmas cards on the bookshelves and mention the exciting details in Angela and Graham's Christmas round robin letter – Angela's degree in athletics, Graham's new boat and their trip to Cannes – and our mother might say, 'Who gives a fuck?' gather up the cards and hide them.

Our mother confounded us. On the one hand, she claimed to absolutely *love* Christmas, on the other, there were only about three things she didn't hate. Firstly and mainly the music, secondly all the holly and ever-greenery (she'd scramble up treacherous railway embankments to get the best and most heavily berried holly) and thirdly her Swedish chiming Angel-abra. It was very important to assemble this apparatus every year but the truth was it didn't work – the turbine never got hot enough to power the trumpet-holding angels so they never 'flew' and therefore never struck the bells beneath. My mother would help it along with surreptitious strokes but then it might chime too quickly or collapse into a heap of smutty brass angel parts. Still, she liked it. Everything else was a huge chore and a pain in the neck. The biggest pain, of course, being the turkey (as previously mentioned, many times).

The turkey — gigantic, ill-looking, plucked, not quite defrosted, not yet basted — would be sitting in a large roasting tin on the downstairs toilet (it being too big for the real fridge and the downstairs toilet being as cold as a fridge). We might tease our mother about the turkey being on the toilet for a while — it being traditional to do so — and maybe take a photograph of it with the Domestos in the background. And then I might pause and reflect that, not so long ago, that poor turkey had been pecking corn somewhere to the east and now it was dead and that my mother was on her grim annual quest for Christmas perfection and yet there we were — being disrespectful all round — and un-Christmassy.

By teatime on Christmas Eve, our mother — noting that a game of Cluedo and a lot of chocolate had overstimulated us — might forcefully suggest we go down to the pub, leaving her in peace to lean on the worktop in her underlit kitchen, listening to Henry Purcell, making lists in multicoloured felt pens and planning her attack on the turkey. I've seen her do this many times — the Sedgwicks' flashing CRIMBO staining her hand and the paper and the side of her face momentarily red, on and off, on and off, as if there was some kind of emergency.

At the village pub, the Christmas trip home would turn into a sort of annual stocktake where we'd evaluate our current lives – in London, in my case – against the ones we'd left behind. I'd see all my old colleagues, the friends I missed, the few I'd dumped – their hair, jeans and jackets and their husbands (that I might have had) – and I'd note the fact that they still all had each other. I might bump into friends who'd also come home for Christmas. These friends might have brought a handsome, foreign-speaking partner back with them, or a new hairdo, or exciting anecdotes about working with Brian Eno, adapting a Truman Capote novella, or horse riding across Argentina. And being university educated they might say something about the 'going home at Christmas hell' being an important human experience that we should all share, and not taking part being tantamount to shooting a monkey (bad luck) or being a loner (scary) or being a Scrooge (bad).

I might meet my old best friend and her daughter – allowed in for a quick lemonade before bed, because it's Christmas Eve – and this child might look so exactly like her mother did at that age that I'd want to sob for all the brilliant, ridiculous times we had – the boys on mopeds, the clothes and make-up, discos at the working men's club, skiving off school, the awful things our parents did (especially mine), the joy of making nuisance phone calls to the racists she'd accidentally babysat for, and the time we almost fell out because she was having regular, full sex with my boyfriend (but I didn't mind because I wanted her as my friend more than I liked him). But it was so, so long ago and she's all grown up now and busy and proper and barely remembers any of it. But I'm not, and I *do* remember.

And then, with that all out of the way, the next morning, Christmas would really begin.

We'd start being helpful – I might make the bread sauce with clove-infused milk, while chatting, and I might even lend someone my Sellotape. And we'd have the Christmas dinner, the table gift torches, the walk, the telly.

And it would be wonderful.

It always seemed like the last resort at the time – going home for Christmas – as though there was something else (possibly abroad, in a new coat and fluffy boots) we should or could be doing but hadn't quite risen to, on our own. But there we were, as always.

The funny thing is, though, of all the Christmases I've had since – the ones with my own captivated little children, the Alpine ski holidays, skating in Central Park – it's those trips home to that hot, crowded, chaotic house and village pub that feel like Christmas proper, with my Christmas-phobic mum, her chiming angels and the turkey on the toilet.

CHRISTMAS SHOPPING

I'm not usually the sort to claim expertise on anything — even the things I actually am an expert on, such as bicycle gears, horse breeds and what people are really thinking — and I'm amazed at how many of my friends write and talk with seeming authority, for money, about subjects they know nothing about. But there is one thing I'm happy to advise on, and that's Christmas presents. And the only reason I haven't put out a book called *Gifts & Gifting at Xmas: A Busy Person's Guide* is because I'm in my fifties and I've had it drummed into me since I was born that the real meaning of Christmas is *not* the presents.*

I just *am* very good at Christmas shopping, and anyone who knows me will eventually admit it. This talent first showed itself when I was a small child and somehow knew that my mother would prefer a bottle of whisky to any other thing you could get in a village (apart from a hand-carved garden bench – which was beyond my budget) and knowing this, I went to the off-licence hatch in the pub and got her a small bottle of Bell's. She drank it straight down and thanked me for not getting her the usual glass animal or fruit soap. Later, during my teen years, and with a December birthday, I became an adept re-gifter. And then, once I had a bit of cash to spend, I really hit my stride. My highlight – and the best gift I've given to date – came in 1992 when I picked the boss's name (Vincent Cassidy) out of the hat for the departmental Secret Santa and, with a £3 upper limit and a whole lunch hour to shop, I triumphed. The boss was overjoyed with *The Laughter and Tears of a Cockney Sparrow* – the biography of Barbara Windsor – and I was immediately over-promoted and went on to a glittering career in academic book publishing. So, you see, it pays to gift well.

---

* Also, I've had it drummed into me never to say 'gifting' but I allow myself because of 're-gifting'.

The real meaning of Christmas is, of course, the birth (and subsequent goodness) of Jesus and being nice to less fortunate neighbours in his honour. And the presents are nowhere near as important. However, if – like me – you have a huge, materialistic family and/or a circle of fairly shallow friends, it's probable that you find Christmas shopping slightly overwhelming as well as expensive, time-consuming, financially ruinous, worrying and stressful. Because of this – and because of all the woeful, wrong, pointless presents I see, year after year – I will force myself to tackle the subject, trusting that you don't need me to dwell on the true meaning because you already know the details.

Christmas shopping has always been a headache, certainly going back as far as the 1970s, when I remember all the desperate adults wishing they'd paid more into their Christmas club, had fewer children, or not spent so much on package holidays in the summer. But the thing is, nowadays, it's so much more than just the money.

It's not just the time it takes, either. What it really is (nowadays) is performance anxiety brought on by so much choice and the modern-day quest for kudos. Not only do we want to get our friends and relatives a present, we want them to like it and admire us for finding it.

Television advertising illustrates this. Where, in the olden days, we saw the gift item displayed, plus price tag and the word 'bargain' in a star shape, we now have to see a close-up of the person being handed the gift. The slow-motion gasp as they fling their arms around the giver and smile, with tears swelling in their blinking eyes.

The quest for kudos causes certain people (with not enough to do) to go to extraordinary lengths to satisfy – especially if they're going to be with the recipient on the day and can really bask in the glory and possibly appear on Instagram or Twitter with the person's arms flung around them and captioned #BestGiftEvah #BestSista – thus raising the gifting bar higher and higher and making it all the harder for the rest of us.

Also guilty are the Christmas gift sections that appear in the colour supplements in mid-December – featuring pages of nice stuff that pretty much anyone would love but that ordinary people like me didn't used to even know about and could be oblivious to. But now it's right there – at your breakfast table or flashing up on your device. Here's the thing, though, these features come out approximately eight weeks too late. You can't get that quirky Lego-shaped cushion from the pop-up, online cushion shop for your nephew because a) you've already got him some gloves from M&S which, albeit seeming so dull now, did cost a fiver, and b) the ethical online retailer will be completely sold out of every-thing due to being featured in the supplement. And the papers daren't run these gift features any earlier because, if they did, a key influencer might post a sarcastic tweet saying:

OMFG, @guardian is floggin Xmas sh*te already #Noooooo #XmasinOctober #TooSoon #Boycott #SorryElton.

What not to get

I see people fall into the same time/money-wasting traps, year after year. I have fallen into those traps myself but, unlike others (I shan't name names), I have learned by these mistakes.

>> Don't be overgenerous, or mean or give precedent-setting gifts.
>> Just because you like a thing, it doesn't mean anyone else will.
>> Go for suitability and proper niceness over quirk or gift kudos.
>> Never give cigarettes or toothpaste unless the person is in prison.

Crazes

Fads, trends, crazes make bad gifts (especially if you do your Christmas shopping early). I have wasted literally thousands of pounds on these. I bought a ton of GoGos, two dozen Dingbats, a pair of Flubes and, two years ago (or, crikey, was it three years ago?) all the Loom Bandz kits I could lay my hands on . . . and by the time I gave them either the fad was over, or the kid had so many of the things s/he didn't want to see one ever again. Or there was a new version, or a new thing, and it was just awkward. I'm writing this knowing that many people will never have known what most of these were. And those who did have probably forgotten.

High-maintenance gifts

A silver charm bracelet is a lovely idea, and it means you don't have to think about your god-daughter's gift ever again. You can keep buying tiny pairs of scissors and horse heads until you die. But, in reality, the kid loses it almost immediately (for example, it falls down a crack between the floorboards in the hall, where some wires also go, and without lifting the floorboards, etc.). Of course the godmother keeps sending charms, year after year, to add to the bracelet and these get put in a pants drawer but, because they're not fixed on to an actual bracelet, they get lost, too. And whenever the godmother comes to the house she keeps glancing at the kid's wrist, and it's all very awkward.

Upsetting gifts

Don't start a funeral plan for anyone or buy them a carpet shampooer. Death and hard work are un-Christmassy and upsetting.

Unusual gifts

My old friend Jay tells about how he was once given a tiny slice of the Atlantic Ocean for Christmas. It was somewhere near Boston and had no coastline abutting, but it was his and he had a certificate to say so. It was a choppy bit of sea and, although he took a boat out to it, he was never entirely sure he was home, even using his TomTom. He did see a whale in the distance one time – and since then has wondered whether the whale sighting wasn't actually the real gift? Charming but frustrating.

Bulking up

A common, expensive, precedent-setting mistake. My mother used to add a *Mr Men* book, a dragon-shaped eraser and a novelty sweetie of some kind to bulk up gifts to her grandchildren. All added up, this meant she'd spend somewhere in the region of a thousand pounds just on bulker-uppers. Bulker-uppers are never a good idea. As well as the cost, including the environmental cost, there's the awful truth that the bulking items – the Kinder egg, the Rimmel nail polish, the fridge magnet of David Hockney's sausage dog, Stanley – are often so much nicer than the actual box of *Star Wars* Lego or the biography of Nick Clegg. Stop bulking up – it's the antithesis of Christmas.

It has just occurred to me that the book you're now reading might well be a bulker-upper.

Event gifts

I'm not against these per se. Just a few words. Going to the theatre is a huge treat, of course. We have enjoyed gift tickets for *Oliver!*, *War Horse* and *Oliver!* again. Last year, I asked the person giving us tickets for *School of Rock* if we might upgrade from the medium to the good seats. And even though I offered to pay the difference and forgo dinner and a bulking-up gift – and the gifter seemed more than happy – somehow news of my upgrade request spread around the family as (further) evidence of my fussiness. But, as I have now explained many times, these 'event gifts' come at great cost when the event venue is a ten-hour round trip on the train (more if you include the replacement bus service) and requires an overnight stay either in an expensive hotel or at a friend's house on the Mile End Road. So, if you do give tickets, pay the extra in lieu of dinner or a Kinder egg.

The formula or repeat

You know this person likes dolphins or Pam Ayres or Chuck Berry or once went to the Chelsea Flower Show and you buy to that formula, year after year after year. My dog-loving sister has apparently received the film *Best in Show* six times from the same three people (including me). I have three copies of *The Hidden Places of Cornwall* and enough *Alan Bennett Diaries* to build an extension. Basically, if the idea is *that* good, someone else will probably already have thought of it – perhaps even the person themselves.

Charity

Although I approve heartily of these gifts by proxy – my father and his wife have for years given people goats, bicycles, schoolbooks and water purification equipment on other people's behalf – I must alert you to the fact that there is exactly the same hierarchy (and cross-family comparisons) as there is with 'real' gifts. One year, one of my children received a flock of young chickens plus materials for a chicken coop for a village in Malawi. The other got notice of some life-saving vaccines. This was the gift equivalent of a blister pack of Nurofen versus a flock of adorable baby chicks and cute little henhouse.

Vouchers

Practical and sensible, but vouchers are just not Christmassy and afford no joy. I'd go as far as to say I hate giving (or getting) any kind of token or voucher. And no matter how much thought you've put into them (joke), they seem lazy and dull. You can get quality ones, but these can misfire. A friend once gave me a voucher for a full-body massage and tummy tickle at a hotel. After Christmas, I lied to my friend and said I'd really enjoyed the experience. Then, the hotel sent a chasing email, telling my friend the voucher *had not been redeemed* and was about to expire. And so my friend chased *me* and asked why I hadn't redeemed the voucher, and why I'd lied. I said, 'Not everyone wants a teenager on the minimum wage pummelling them.' It was humiliating all round – and that was without even going.

So, on the whole, I'm saying vouchers are un-Christmassy. The only exceptions being some kind of weird marriage proposal/sex voucher. Or a personal pledge to clean the car, inside and out, including door surrounds.

What to get

I have a huge, never-ending family. I have a father, a stepfather, a father-in-law. A mother, a stepmother, two mothers-in-law. I have a best friend, a best friend's husband and their kid. I have a kid who's convinced I'm his godmother and always demands money from me. I have two brothers and their partners and kids, wives and ex-wives, a second best friend and his dog. I have a sister, her kids, her dogs, her husband, his kids, their dogs, her parents-in-law. I have two half-sisters who have six children and one dog each, two half-brothers and their wives and kids. This all adds up to almost a thousand people who all deserve lovely, thoughtful gifts.

In recent years, some of my family – me included – have begun to find the sheer numbers involved plus other awful aspects of shopping (discussed above) anxiety- and anger-inducing in the run-up to Christmas. Not wishing to start shuffling banknotes or, God forbid, vouchers around the family, we have tried various burden-lightening strategies, to save time, promote fairness, stop our children and dogs getting too much rubbish, and help them remember the true meaning of Christmas. You might want to try some of the following for yourselves.

Useful gifts

One year, I think about 2001, the rule was that all gifts had to be genuinely useful. I bought people glove compartment motoring atlases (it was before we all had maps on our phones) and, for non-drivers, mini first-aid kits to keep under the sink in case of kitchen accidents. My gifts got very little acknowledgement because my friend Stella deliberately misinterpreted the word 'useful' and got everyone nail varnish or, for those who couldn't be trusted with it, goat-milk hand cream. That was my least Christmassy Christmas ever because, apart from my goat-milk hand cream, I received a multi-headed screwdriver and a device to loosen tight lids on jam jars, both of which were slightly overshadowed by the bunion relief kit.

'I haven't got a bunion,' I told my sister.

'You have – on the right foot,' she said.

'Is that a bunion?'

'Yes, left unchecked that's going to put paid to sandal wearing,' she warned.

Someone gave my sister vouchers for a registered window cleaner, which – though not Christmassy – I'd have loved, but she didn't (she always did her own since a window cleaner had freaked out her dogs with a noisy squeegee on a pole).

Books only

I think it was 2006 we first agreed on a 'books only' policy. I got a plus size dictionary and *Tim the Tiny Horse* by Harry Hill. And my daughter, thirty-something years younger than me, got the same two books, plus a box of dates. A few years later – 2011, I think – we did 'books only' again, and this time Jamie Oliver's *30-Minute Meals* cleaned up. I gave five copies of *How to be a Woman* by Caitlin Moran, five copies of *David Copperfield* and was branded 'lazy'.

Food and drink

The year 2007 was 'food and drink only'. Some gave biscuits, cakes and smoked salmon, others gave chocolates, Christmassy pickles and jams. All went down very well and we tucked in. The annoying thing was, though, I'd spent just as much if not more than everyone else but have since come to terms with the fact that, however genuine and expensive – and no matter how many appellations or how long it's had brewing in an old oak cask – kudos-wise, vinegar is tantamount to panettone.

The Christmas amnesty

The proposed amnesty in 2003 was very much favoured by the busiest members of the family (and the most miserly). I was very much for it but we amnesty-mongers were shouted down and called 'Scrooges'. I was annoyed about this because the loudest cries came from a sibling who never actually managed to send anything – and if she did you'd have to drive to a depot somewhere to pay the excess postage charges and get a dirty look from the postal worker. We agreed to buy nothing except for children under eighteen. My two children did rather well that year. But I have to confess that Vic and I secretly broke the amnesty and bought each other lovely jewellery gifts. And between us got my mum a coffee-making machine and two mugs from Powys Castle to bulk it up. Somehow, one of our brothers found the gift tags and we were rumbled.

Re-gifting

Re-gifting used to go uncommented upon until we all started photographing everything for the world to see. In my expert opinion it's a legitimate and even exciting part of the giving and receiving. Some gifts, such as the Powys Castle mugs,* go round and round. A true re-gifter is able to mentally re-gift upon opening and will happily store away horrible gifts until next year, or put them on eBay – asap – with original packaging.

Home-made

The worst year was the year of the home-made food gifts. It was bad enough that people kept giving plastic bags full of gravelly fudge or untrustworthy cheese straws. One person made everyone a single, albeit deep-filled, mince pie. *One* mince pie. My offerings

---

* These were acquired from a bargain barrel in a gift shop in North Wales as a bulker-upper and soon became the most travelled stoneware since the Midland Railway opened its Ripley Branch. To receive the Powys Castle mugs is to feel initially disappointed and unvalued, and even hated, but then to come to your senses and realize that you're actually very loved indeed. This is how I handle it, anyway.

were well-intentioned failures. I transferred catering olives into glass jars and added lemon slices, sprigs of herbs and the odd chilli — all made and bottled and nicely tagged by early December. On Christmas Day I had a series of phone calls from people pretending they wanted to wish us Merry Christmas but really just wanting to say that my olives had gone mouldy and now their house stank.

Promises

This was 2012. The promises — ranging from manicures to fridge cleaning — mostly came to nothing. Some due to bad publicity: I never claimed my pedicure after hearing of one that had ended in blood and tears. Some for logistical reasons: my friend Rebecca didn't claim her hour of cognitive behavioural therapy that I'd promised, because my father was the only person qualified and I hadn't included the train fare to Wolverhampton where he lived. So I did it instead — and heard about her fear of plant pots and getting hairs in her lipgloss. And some for more sociological reasons: a friend and I were promised front-door facelifts (two coats of gloss and undercoat, not including the cost of the paint and Brasso) from my brother-in-law. My friend claimed hers first and it was a triumph, literally adding thousands to the value of her house. By the time my turn came around my sister and brother-in-law had started divorce proceedings, and though it was amicable, and I really wanted a rejuvenated door, I reluctantly agreed to waive the debt.

PS: This year we are 'free range', which will be nice. I'm giving Loom Bandz kits to everyone, having found my stash from 2013.

'MERRY XMAS EVERYBODY'

I honestly can't remember what makes me think of throwing a Christmas party, it just pops into my head one day — fairy lights in the porch, Glue Vine and mince pies, Christmas carols playing in the background, and a few dogs snoozing on washable blankets. It's such a nice idea that I immediately text an invitation to everyone I know, in town, plus my friends — Deborah and Miss Yates — who are twenty-three and fifteen miles away respectively but very worth having, and the St Ives Frearses — who can be one hundred per cent relied upon to enjoy themselves.

And they all text straight back, saying they'd love to come. I'm thrilled.

Then, after a slight mood swing, I ring my sister Vic, who is three hundred miles away but a Christmas lover, and suggest she might schedule her annual shopping trip to Lakeland, Truro to coincide with a Christmas party I'm thinking of having. She's keen to do some shopping all right, but advises me to drop the idea of having a Christmas party because of the enormous amount of hard work involved that she can't see me enjoying. She reminds me, unnecessarily, that she's masterminded two weddings (her own), two christenings and a funeral, one of them in a foreign country, whereas I have no experience of organizing anything except one chip supper where we all sat on the slabs outside Rick Stein's and looked at the view.

'But this'll just be a simple, no-fuss tea,' I reassure her.

'There's no such thing,' she says, 'and saying "no-fuss tea" you reveal your ignorance and naivety.'

It's too late – I confess – I've already invited fifty people and their dogs and spouses.

She makes a whistling noise down the phone.

Vic arrives a day and a half before the party and her managerial experience shows immediately. She points out that party guests might expect more than just a mini mince pie and a Rich Tea at a Christmas party.

'OK,' I say, 'I'll buy a cake.'

We clash over the beverages. I tell her I've been imagining a steaming cauldron of Glue Vine with whole spices and citrus fruits on the hob. Vic agrees an overpowering smell of cloves and cinnamon can be a blessing, but predicts that people will want endless cups of tea and, therefore, do I own enough cups? And so forth.

I hand over control and a £35 budget and she recruits my two teenage offspring as unpaid interns.

She makes a chart on a large whiteboard, listing in capital letters all the things we need to do, buy and bake:

CLEAN WHOLE HOUSE
HIDE JUNK
HIDE VALUABLES
MOVE XMAS TREE
HIDE LAUNDRY
BATHE DOG
BATHROOM CLEAN
WINDOW SNOWFLAKES
BISCUITS
150+ MINCE PIES
FIRST-AID KIT

She's like a strict supply teacher and we're the challenging pupils suddenly brought to heel. She assigns the work by adding initials to each task, and

I can't help noticing 'NS' scribbled beside 150+ MINCE PIES and BATHROOM CLEAN.

'We've only got a twelve-pie baking tray – shall I do them in batches, or run down to Lakeland for more trays?'

'Use your initiative,' says Vic.

'What would you do, though, in my shoes?' I ask.

'I'd have had them made – ready-to-bake – and refrigerated by . . . no, I'd never find myself in your shoes.'

'Do we *have* to have mince pies?' I ask.

'It's entirely up to you,' says Vic, 'your party.'

I begin to hate that she keeps referring to it as 'my party' and remind her that we are sisters, we're in it together, forever. She strongly suggests I get cracking with the pastry.

'Right! Is there anything else to add to this to-do list?' Vic asks.

And, before I can stop myself, I shout, 'Christmas music!'

And the other three respond, in unison, 'I'll do the music.'

Vic writes PLAYLIST on the whiteboard.

'No, it's OK – *I'll* do the music. I've got a Christmas playlist,' I lie.

Vic ignores me and scribbles VJG (which are very much *her* initials) on the whiteboard beside PLAYLIST.

I cough, point and exchange a look with the kids. I repeat, 'I have a Christmas playlist already,' and notice *Vic* cough and exchange a look with the kids.

'I don't think we should let Mum be in charge,' says one of them, 'she listens to music by putting her phone inside an empty jug.'

The other one defends me. 'Vic's Angry Birds speaker is no better than Mum's jug.'

'Never mind the device, please can we collaborate on the actual songs,' Vic says, 'otherwise we'll be stuck with gloomy old carols all afternoon – and I don't think I could stand it.'

A discussion ensues.

Vic and the kids agree to listen to my (currently non-existent) Christmas playlist and then add Christmassy favourites that the guests (who Vic keeps referring to as 'your doggie mates') will enjoy. Unsurprisingly, we can't seem to agree on what people's Christmassy favourites actually are.

My son has reasonable taste (compared to the other two), but his only real concession to Christmas is John and Yoko. My daughter favours weird, indie stuff that might alienate my older friends and make them think there are drugs going round. Vic wants the usual crowd-pleasers, and no one mentions a single carol except 'Away in a Manger' (which Vic loves because of the cattle lowing and the baby awake but behaving himself). The one thing the three of them agree on is that 'Merry Xmas Everybody' by Slade is the best Christmas song ever written and everyone's Christmas favourite.

I think about 'Merry Xmas Everybody' by Slade and I'm not sure it *is* the best Christmas song ever written. Of course I *used* to love it. I used to *really* love it. We all did. But it's so overplayed, and always played too soon. It's been ruined. There are a hundred better songs.

I begin a half-hearted search for pie-making ingredients and suddenly feel I must make a start on my imaginary playlist and, on the spur of the moment, I invent an imminent conference call with the USA to buy myself some time.

'A *conference call*,' says Vic, '*now?*'

'Yes, they just want a quick catch-up,' I lie.

'Really! What time is it in New York?' asks Vic.

'Almost seven a.m.,' says my daughter, who annoyingly knows these things.

'They're calling you at *seven a.m.*?' says Vic.

'They start work early in the run-up to Christmas,' I say.

'So they can leave early and get their mince pies made,' says my daughter.

'Good for them,' says Vic.

She's genuinely impressed by this, and I'm genuinely proud of my US colleagues and their imaginary early starts and pies. Vic recommends that I don't let the US team 'ramble on endlessly' and that I crack on with the pastry as soon as I've got them off the line.

I agree. 'Yes, I'll be back in a few minutes and we can listen to my playlist while I crack on with the pies,' I say, and run upstairs.

It's not that I'm a massive music control freak (any more than anyone else), but I don't want to leave it entirely to Vic and the kids because – to be honest – I don't trust them. I want a largely carol-based list. I don't want anyone getting carried away to one of Vic's rock anthems after a Glue Vine and a pie. Or if they do get carried away, it ought to at least be in a Christmassy way.

I log into Spotify. I find I'm nostalgic for the olden days when Christmas music meant rotating two or three CDs (say, *Carols from King's* or, if a more popular mood is required, *Motown Christmas Gold* or, for easy listening, *Geoff Love's Christmas*) and there'd be no scrutinizing, no stress, no trying to collaborate or seize control. And I conclude that Christmas music – like Christmas shopping – has become stressful due to a combination of infinite choice and the quest for cool.

I create a new playlist called 'Nina's Christmas Playlist' and search for 'Christmas carols' and, sure enough, every carol I've ever heard is available in a never-ending list: performed traditionally, jazzed up, crooned, trilled, belted and thrashed out by folksters, pop stars, rock stars, megastars and Sting. I don't know which to choose. I don't know what I like any more. I find some ready-made Christmas playlists — compiled by Christmas music aficionados — but even the good ones are contaminated with unbearable songs. Such as, 'It's the Most Wonderful Time of the Year' by Andy Williams, which is undeniably delightful but always makes me think of the worst kind of disaster (someone choking on a bauble or a laughing person being carted off in a straitjacket).

The phone rings — it's my dog-walking friend Nancy. She's ringing to ask if it's OK if she brings Richard to the party.

'Richard?' I say. 'Do I know him?'

'Yes,' she says, 'you know, the one with the wire-haired pointer — you always refer to him as "Butch".'

'Oh, yes, Butch,' I say, and tell her of course she can bring him.

I describe to Nancy the struggle for music control that's unfolding.

She tuts. She's just had a similar thing at the dog training Christmas supper, where a male helper/music-lover (Butch?) has repeatedly overridden the Christmas favourites queued on her modest device and subjected them to endless Chuck Berry and The Big Bopper via his Music Flow.

'What *are* your favourites?' I ask.

'You know, "Silent Night", "Hark the Herald" — that type of thing.'

'Exactly,' I say. And, while she rambles, I search 'Silent Night'.

I listen to many different versions, after which I feel a bit gloomy and realize I don't like 'Silent Night'. And the more versions I hear, the worse it gets. I find myself a) annoyed with Nancy for suggesting it, but at the same time b) determined to find a bearable one for her – after being overridden by a music bully.

I hear it by various choirs, by Presley, Bieber, Sinatra, Rod Stewart, SuBo, Bublé, Nat King Cole, Eva Cassidy, Miley Cyrus, Annie Lennox, Jim Reeves, Aretha, Sinéad O'Connor, Leona Lewis, Aaron Lewis, Phil Spector, Mary J. Blige, Neil Diamond, Simon and Garfunkel, The Temptations, Carpenters, Destiny's Child, Bros, Mahalia Jackson, The Staple Singers, CeeLo Green, Stevie Nicks, and Sidney Bechet. The only one I don't dislike is the Mary J. Blige but I drag all of them on to 'Nina's Christmas Playlist', which I will edit later, leaving just the best one.

It's obviously not an easy song to pull off – the monotonous solo, the high notes, the low notes, the long notes, the obvious, desperate-sounding struggle for breath and the notes that change key – even the most accomplished singers must dread it and thank God there are only three verses. Personally, I never want to hear it again.

I move on. I find that – even counting 'Silent Night' – the *real* test for a pro-singer is 'Hark the

Herald Angels Sing'. And, I hate to say it but not even Queen Aretha can make anything of it. I listen to around twelve versions and can't stand it any more. Only a version by Johnny Cash makes it on to 'Nina's Christmas Playlist'.

I add a traditional version of 'O Come, All Ye Faithful' because my friend Sam apparently loves it. And I'm about to embark on 'In the Bleak Midwinter' when my phone pings. A text message from Vic reads: 'RU done with yr Americans? Need to crack on w pastry.'

I've used up quite a bit of my pie-making time. Back downstairs, I hear music coming from the kitchen. I go in and find 'Dominick the Donkey' playing quite loud and not a single thing crossed off the to-do list.

'I thought you were making chocolate biscuits and snowflaking the windows and cleaning the whole house,' I say.

'We've been compiling a list of songs to add to your playlist,' they say, defensively.

And there it is, on the whiteboard, in a mixture of handwriting. It goes something like this, but longer:

'Merry Xmas Everybody' – Slade
'Away in a Manger'
'Carol of the Bells'
'Fairytale of New York' – The Pogues and Kirsty McColl

'Last Christmas' – Wham!

'Walking in the Air' – Aled Jones

'Twist and Shout' – The Beatles

'Blue Christmas' – Elvis

'Happy Xmas (War Is Over)' – John and Yoko

'Dominick the Donkey'

'Rudolf the Red-Nosed Reindeer' – Ella Fitzgerald

'Let it Snow' – Ella

'Frosty the Snowman' – Ella

'All I Want for Christmas Is You' – Mariah Carey

'Everything's Gonna Be Cool This Christmas' – Eels

'I'll Find My Way Home' – Jon and Vangelis

'Santa Claus Is Coming to Town' – The Jackson 5

'In the Bleak Midwinter' – Dame Kiri Te Kanawa

'Merry Xmas Everybody' – Slade

'2000 Miles' – The Pretenders

'Hells Bells' – AC/DC

'Lonely This Christmas' – Mud

'O Holy Child' – Dusty Springfield

'Mary's Boy Child' – Boney M.

'O Tannenbaum' – Nat King Cole

'Joy to the World' – Johnny Cash

'The Blizzard' – Camera Obscura

'Have Yourself a Merry Little Christmas' – Lou Rawls

'Jingle Bells' – Count Basie

'The Little Drummer Boy' – Stevie Wonder

'White Christmas' – Bing Crosby

I can't find anything really wrong with it – except there aren't enough Christmas carols, and I worry that 'Twist and Shout' could give people ideas (dancing). I agree to add them on to 'Nina's Christmas Playlist'. As an aside, I question 'Merry Xmas Everybody' by Slade – is it *really* everyone's favourite Christmas song ever? And does it need to be on twice?

'You *love* Slade – I know you do,' says Vic, and she drifts into a strange, implausible and unnecessarily long anecdote about hearing it one time when she was being given medical assistance after being stung on the face by a jellyfish.

'So, what's on *your* playlist?' asks my son.

' "Silent Night", "Hark the Herald" and stuff like that,' I say.

The three of them look dismayed.

Vic claps her hands and tells us that, 'Due to musical distractions, we're woefully behind schedule,' and we must now prioritize.

She asks if I've got my pastry made and chilling in non-PVC cling film, which she knows I haven't because I've been nowhere near the kitchen.

'Those mince pies aren't going to get made,' she says.

'You're right,' I say, 'I'll crack on.'

'No,' says Vic, 'I mean, they're *really* not going to get made.'

'Shall I dash and buy them?'

'I would, in your shoes,' she says.

In M&S there are many varieties of mince pie on offer. A helpful assistant shows which ones I can most easily pass off as home-made (non-fluted, shallow). She reminds me to remove the little foil containers, rough them up a bit, warm them and dust them with icing sugar before serving.

Back at home, I get one of the kids to add their list of songs on to 'Nina's Christmas Playlist' while I place the 132 pies in a huge plastic box, hide the foil containers in the recycling and begin my BATHROOM CLEAN.

The party is in full swing; I can barely hear the music because of the noise of the kettle constantly being boiled for endless pots of tea. And then, later, I can hear it but I'm not paying much attention, due to the braying voices in what Vic calls 'UKIP corner'.

Making more tea, I hear the opening of Bublé's 'Silent Night'. I hope Nancy can hear it. I laugh because I meant to leave the Blige version, not the Bublé, on the playlist. Still, it's nice enough.

'Ooh, "Silent Night"!' says my neighbour.

'Bublé,' I say.

'Is it?' he asks.

'Yes, definitely,' I say, 'I'm an expert on "Silent Night".'

The neighbour grimaces. 'I think we all are.'

I notice Nancy and Butch and their dogs about to leave. I see them to the door and we chat for a moment. Butch is a bit tipsy.

'Lovely party,' says Nancy.

'I hope you heard "Silent Night",' I say, 'I put it on the playlist especially for you.'

'Yes, I heard it,' she says, 'it was lovely.'

Butch is trying to say something but Nancy bundles him out of the door and into the night. 'Bye, thanks, Merry Christmas!' Nancy calls.

Later, I'm circulating with another tray of tea and I hear the opening bars of 'Merry Xmas Everybody' by Slade and I see everyone begin to sway and almost imperceptibly move their heads. I realize that I *adore* it. And that I never stopped loving it. We've drifted apart – me and the song – that's all. It's like having slipped out of love with the perfect husband, or wife, just out of laziness and taking them for granted. Or having lost touch with a dear, wonderful friend, who has accidentally won the pools. I've let myself become irritated by its success and popularity. It hasn't felt as though it belonged to me any more. It has seemed that it belongs to everyone else. It is ubiquitous. It is over-played. It's played too soon. But it *is* my favourite of all Christmas songs. It makes me feel so happy. And Christmassy.

It's who we were, who we are. It's Wolverhampton and the Midlands and the whole country in the shit but not going to give up and not going to wallow but looking to the future. It's Noddy Holder being funny and extraordinary and ordinary. And I'm proud of Vic for loving it. She's talking to June, one of my doggie mates, about dry, cracked paw pads.

I interrupt. 'You're right,' I say, 'I *do* love this song – I adore it.'

'I know you do,' says Vic, 'but not as much as you like "Silent Night".'

She and June laugh.

'What d'you mean?' I ask.

'We've had fifteen "Silent Nights" so far tonight,' says Vic. 'I'm getting to quite like it.'

A PRESENT FOR TEACHER: A Story

The last day of school at Christmas was always nice. Each class would take down their Christmas displays and fold them neatly for next year's class and put them into the long thin drawer marked ADVENT in the cabinets that lined the corridors.

After that we'd play board games. I recall that year, 1972, our teacher Mrs Greenwood had a cup of tea at this point with a slice of square fruitcake balanced in the saucer. It seems implausible, but that was Mrs Greenwood for you.

All through infants and juniors our class had the

extra bonus of David, who was unusual – both very clever and babyish at the same time – and whose mother always sent in a tin of Quality Street for the class to share. David, like a real-life Father Christmas, would remember who'd been nice to him and who hadn't as he passed the sweets around. And I always had, and got to sort through to my favourite, because he'd been to my house and stroked our animals and never forgotten it.

Just before games commenced, Mrs Greenwood told us our optional holiday project was to be a short essay on the new Poet Laureate, which we might illustrate with pencil and crayon sketches (but *not* felt-tip pen). Mrs Greenwood always made it clear this work was not only optional but especially meant for the girls – because the boys would probably be playing football or building a model, plus she very much preferred the girls and their work, which was pretty and nice to read. She seemed to find the boys grotty and was always telling them not to cough or yawn or scratch. And if they did, you could see her lip curl.

If we weren't inspired by the new Poet Laureate, we could write a 'My Christmas' instead, but it had to be an imaginary 'My Christmas' – written from someone else's point of view – not our own. The more imaginative the better, she said.

I would do the optional homework. I was a busy

child with a pony, lots of siblings, a dog and a mother trying out new tranquillizers who hated having us around the house, and I certainly didn't need homework to keep me occupied. I'd squeeze it in, though, because I was diligent and eager to please. Added to which, I was particularly keen to make amends for the previous homework (the 'Newspaper' I'd produced during the October half-term break), which Mrs Greenwood had found *abhorrent* (her word) and had flung into the waste-paper basket and then got it out again at playtime and gone to consult with the headmistress.

Mrs Greenwood joined in with our games session heartily. She didn't sit at her desk writing her Christmas cards, like other teachers did at this time. She loved board games and was especially good at draughts, Go and Mastermind.

'I'm a ludic person,' she called out. 'Who can tell me what "ludic" means? Hands up.'

No one put their hand up, so she told us. It meant she had a games-brain – and that was why her husband's inability to play was so peeving.

'Anyone of us in this room could beat Mr G. at Scrabble since his breakdown,' she said, 'including you, David.'

After games, we children exchanged cards, and those who had Christmas gifts for Mrs Greenwood took them to her desk, one at a time, where she

ceremoniously opened them. That year Mrs Greenwood had upset my mother terribly by blacking us up
for the nativity play and then, when she complained
afterwards, mispronouncing 'secretary'. And so I
worried that my mother might not allow me to give
Mrs Greenwood a present. But I was wrong.

The boy called David (whose mother sent the
Quality Street and who'd be able to beat Mr G. at
Scrabble) kicked off with a beautiful, much-wrapped
thing. Mrs Greenwood had him sit beside her, cross-
legged on the carpet, while she tackled it. She beamed
as she picked at the Sellotape and told us that end-of-
term games and gifts were always the highlight of
her Christmas.

'Apart from Christmas worship, of course,' she corrected herself, 'and the producing and directing of
this year's negro-spiritual nativity. And the moment,
at about eleven on Christmas morning, when Jesus
was actually born unto the world.'

David's gift eventually turned out to be a tiny
appointment diary with Mrs Greenwood's initials
embossed on the front in gold (JCG). I marvelled at
David's mother knowing her initials but felt very
much that it eclipsed my hyacinth bulb. My mother
told me later that a hyacinth bulb or some pepper-
mints were the most appropriate for a teacher and
that knowing someone's initials and having them
embossed in gold on a diary was intrusive and going

a bit far. Mrs Greenwood hadn't appeared to feel intruded upon at the time; she had seemed captivated, delighted and quite moved and spoke in a great monologue as she leafed through the tiny pages.

'It's marvellous,' she said, turning to David and giving him a slight bow of her head, which I found most meaningful. And I think David did, too, because his two hands fluttered in front of his face and he shifted about on the carpet.

Mrs Greenwood gazed at him and obviously had some thoughts. And she went on to list the benefits of the diary, including all the royal birthdays, saints' days, holidays, information about daylight and moons and telephone numbers for emergencies, and how to speak to the operator or phone the speaking clock, and so on, plus a whole page for the Latin names of trees – such as *Quercus*, which she made us guess – and another two whole pages for her own personal information, which she filled in there and then with the tiny gold pencil that came in a gap behind the spine and had a red tassel.

'Next of kin,' she called out. 'Who knows what "next of kin" means?'

The boy David did and put his hand up – even though he was sitting right beside her grinning.

'David?'

'It's who the police phone up if you're murdered or injured,' he said very slowly, looking at the floor, as if he'd rehearsed the whole thing with his mother, which I think he had. This was probably his Christmas highlight, too.

'Well, yes,' said Mrs Greenwood, 'or if you lose your mind on the way to work and are found at the bus terminus having been to Leicester and back three times.'

A girl called Glynis commented that the diary seemed so full of facts there was hardly any room for Mrs Greenwood to write in her own appointments. Mrs Greenwood said that wouldn't be a problem because she seldom went anywhere due to being the breadwinner and Mr G. being in chronic physical pain and mental anguish, and neither willing nor very able to visit the arts or countryside.

The same girl butted in to ask who Mrs Greenwood's next of kin was.

'In this context, it would be Jennifer Yap,' said Mrs Greenwood.

'Who's that?' we all asked.

'A dear, dear old friend in Loughborough,' said Mrs Greenwood, 'such a lovely person.'

'Will she mind being your next of kin?' I asked, thinking it rather a long trek from Loughborough to our side of the county to collect the dead or injured or deranged Mrs Greenwood (I knew this because my father lived over there and the car journey made me sick every time).

'No, no, Jennifer won't mind – I became her emergency contact in the summer when Mr Yap passed away, so it's tit for tat really.'

'Why isn't Mr G. your next of kin?' we asked.

'How on earth would he get to the hospital or police station?' said Mrs Greenwood. 'He'd never make it on foot, and he's barred from the bus in any case.'

'Blood type!' Mrs Greenwood called out. 'Why do you think it would be useful to include this information here?'

And so on and so forth, until she'd questioned us and filled in the two pages with all her personal emergency information and written in the addresses of her brother in Vancouver and her cousin in Toronto and made a note of the time difference, etc. And, of course, Jennifer Yap of Loughborough.

The next gift was from a shy girl called Joanna. A mini bottle of red wine and muslin pouch of mulling spices.

Mrs Greenwood read out the instructions. 'Add sachet to red wine and heat gently for a festive and warming cup of cheer. Sufficient for two glasses.' She was visibly excited and kept sniffing it. 'How lovely, I shall enjoy this after church on the day,' she said. 'Sadly, Mr G. does not partake because of his belief that red wine in the bloodstream attracts bedbugs – but he'll enjoy the aroma.'

Next, a girl called Debra presented a basket of scrubbed parsnips from the garden and a cluster of decorative seed heads, which were presumably also parsnips. Mrs Greenwood almost fell off her chair. She told us we could have no idea how much this meant to her and seemed quite overcome for a moment but then diverted quickly into an educational talk and told us that the parsnip dated back to Roman times and was much esteemed by one particular emperor – and could we guess which one?

As luck would have it there was a list of Roman emperors right behind Mrs Greenwood's head and we all squinted our eyes and raised a hand.

'Hadrian?' said one boy.

'No, Hadrian wouldn't have liked parsnips,' said Mrs Greenwood.

'Titus?' said another boy.

'He might have, but he wasn't known for it,' said Mrs Greenwood.

'Marcus?' said another.

'Marcus Aurelius?' she said. 'No, I don't think so.'

Lots of hands waggled in the air.

'I'll give you a clue: he was the adopted son of Augustus and died from poisoned figs.' She was enjoying this.

'Augustus?' called out David.

'No calling out, David – no, not Augustus, don't be silly.'

'Tiberius?' said my friend Melody.

'Yes, Melody!' shouted Mrs Greenwood. 'The emperor Tiberius is said to have adored parsnips, which is a lovely thing to know, isn't it?'

'Yes,' said Melody.

'And I'm the same,' smiled Mrs Greenwood as she touched the specimens. 'They're my favourite of the veg.' She looked at Debra and said again, 'My favourite of the veg.'

Soon it was time for my hyacinth bulb, which was potted and wrapped in brown paper with a ribbon. Mrs Greenwood was pleased with it and asked if I knew what colour it was going to be.

Silently I cursed my mother for not bothering to tell me. 'Blue,' I said with confidence.

'Oh, good – the blue has a superior fragrance,' said Mrs Greenwood, searching her teacher's mind for something more educational to say. 'The hyacinth flower originates in the Lebanon,' she trotted out with none of her usual enthusiasm, but picked up steam with, 'and though it comes from hot climes, we can control the timing of its blooming by keeping it in either a warm or a cool position.' Then, looking at me, she said, 'I know the exact spot in the house where its blueness will be shown off to best advantage and Mr G. will enjoy it. He is a big fan of the colour blue.'

'Or, it might be a pink one,' I said.

She didn't hear. 'He's not a big fan of the pink ones, so that's good,' she carried on.

After that, there was a bit of chit-chat about the gifts we were hoping for, and Mrs Greenwood reminded us to give our mothers the Aida cloth samplers we'd made.

Nosy Debra wanted to know what Mrs Greenwood had got for *Mr* Greenwood.

'Oh, nothing yet – he's a devil to buy for,' she said. 'Probably some socks.'

I secretly thought this a bad idea. I knew, from something Mrs Greenwood had said earlier, that Mr G. only ever wore his carpet slippers and so socks would be unnecessary and probably too hot.

And then, class was over and it was the holidays.

I hung back. I felt I should confess to not really knowing the true colour of the hyacinth. I imagined it bursting into flower on Christmas Day, and wanted to prevent disappointment – especially since Mrs Greenwood was bound to mention its future blueness to Mr G. I waited at the back of the class, pretending to tie my laces and saw, through the chair and table legs, Mrs Greenwood wrap the parsnips in the brown paper my hyacinth had come in and slip them into the waste-paper basket.

She looked up a moment afterwards and saw me. 'Oh,' she said, 'it's just that Mr G. absolutely detests parsnips.'

'That's OK,' I said.

She didn't want an argument with him, she explained. Not that he ever said anything, but he'd be put out and he'd worry about it, and she'd know it by his eyes.

'I understand,' I said.

She didn't want them clogging up her bin at home either, over the Christmas period. She could trust me (of all people) to keep it to myself and felt sure I'd understand and not want to hurt Debra's feelings.

And, although I did understand, I heard myself say, 'But parsnips are your favourite of the veg. And they're for you, not him. He doesn't have to partake, he can have peas.'

We remained silent for a while and I thought she was about to cry, but she didn't. She clapped her hands, took the wrapped parsnips out of the bin and put them in her basket, nestled among the other gifts and Christmas cards we'd made her.

'You're right,' she said.

'I just wanted to tell you I'm not actually a hundred per cent sure what colour the hyacinth will be,' I said. 'I was only guessing.'

'Then it'll be a lovely surprise,' said Mrs Greenwood. 'Fingers crossed for blue.'

I began planning my optional Christmas homework in my head as I walked home from school. I wanted it out of the way. I decided quickly against the Poet Laureate. Partly because I'd forgotten how to spell Betjeman, and partly because I'd picked up a slight anti-Betjeman vibe from Mrs Greenwood when she'd described him as 'probably German – but hiding it'. I'd do a 'My Christmas' and make it meaningful, teacher-pleasing and perfect – to make up for the newspaper (mentioned earlier) that had disgusted Mrs Greenwood.

After a few false starts – the literary Christmas ramblings of a Labrador and then the gift hopes of Lady Jane Grey – it came to me.

'My Christmas' by Mr Greenwood

December 24th

What a day! My wife surprised me with a basket of parsnips. To begin with I was furious and if I could speak I would have shouted, 'No, Joan C. Greenwood, not parsnips! You know I wish they'd never been invented.'

But I can't speak so I winked and nodded at my wife in my special language so she got the idea.

Joan was really patient, though, and explained that one of her pupils who lives in a tiny scruffy house (with mushrooms growing on the stairs) had harvested them from her garden, scrubbed them and arranged them in a festive way. I still

shook my head to say, 'No, get them out of here.'
But my dear, kind wife (who is a teacher and
clever at understanding my private language)
wouldn't leave it be. She told me that the
Emperor Tiberius had had them brought from
the Rhine valley to his house in Rome and then
later to his holiday house on the tropical island
of Capri because he liked them so much. I've got
to be honest, that made me think, 'If parsnips
are good enough for a Roman emperor, they're
good enough for a housebound ex-bank manager'
and I blinked this out to Joan and she thanked
me with her eyes. I am lucky to live with such a
good woman.

<u>December 25th</u>
What a day! I used to wish Christmas hadn't
been invented (as well as parsnips) but I've
changed my mind. My wife gave me a beauti-
fully wrapped Christmas present, which I love,
but can't remember now what it was because of
my mental problems, but I do know we went to
church and had a nice Christmas dinner of
chicken and all the trimmings. You might
remember what I wrote yesterday (about parsnips) but I have to say, although they weren't
my cup of tea, it was a joy seeing Mrs Greenwood tucking in. She deserved those parsnips.

After dinner, my dear wife very kindly pushed me around the village in a wheelchair she'd borrowed from Glebe Gardens. We saw many of her pupils and they all called out 'Merry Christmas' because they like her so much and we visited Mr Turner's farm to look at his huge bull called Clay Boy (the father of more than 100 calves). Then, surprise, surprise, my wife's best friend from years ago (Jennifer Yap) turned up and I went to bed so they could have a glass of spiced Christmas wine and catch up on each other's news.

<u>Boxing Day</u>
Great news! The hyacinth is beginning to blossom. Can't quite tell what colour it is yet but I think maybe blue. But I don't mind. I like all colours. As long as it's not pink.

More good news, Jennifer Yap from Loughborough is still here. It turns out she's staying the whole week. She had completely forgotten what a very nice friend Joan is and now doesn't want to go home. Luckily her husband died in the summer so he won't mind. Jennifer Yap is helping around the house and has even helped me with my exercises and has gone round with the Hoover and so on, to give Joan a break. We played Scrabble and Joan beat us both by miles because of her knowledge of millions of tiny words and few big ones. Also, she is strategic whereas Jennifer and I just make the longest words we can, such as 'public' when actually 'clip' would have got a better score. I must say, she certainly does seem to cheer up Mrs G.

After the holidays, Mrs Greenwood asked for any homework to be handed in. Most of the girls and David had done it.

David read out his 'My Christmas' by John Betjeman, which was very funny indeed and had John Betjeman saying he was 'hoping to be a better Poet Laureate than the last clot'.

I didn't hand mine in until after class, just in case I'd misjudged it again.

When I did, I must have looked nervous because Mrs Greenwood said, 'Don't worry, it can't be as bad as last time.'

The next morning, Mrs Greenwood came into the classroom looking a bit pinched. After putting down her bag, she marched up and down the aisles of desks handing back the optional homework to those of us who had bothered.

When she got to me, I looked up and smiled expectantly.

She dropped the paper on my desk without speaking. Mrs Greenwood was usually an enthusiastic marker – lots of ticks, exclamation marks and so forth throughout the text – but there was nothing. Not a word.

I turned it over and, right at the bottom of the page, in her lovely, looping handwriting, she'd written:

The hyacinth was pink. <u>See me</u>.

THE CHRISTMAS TREE

The woods decay, the woods decay and fall,
The vapours weep their burthen to the ground,
Man comes and tills the field and lies beneath,
And after many a summer dies the swan.
Me only cruel immortality
Consumes: I wither slowly in thine arms,
Here at the quiet limit of the world,
A white-hair'd shadow roaming like a dream
The ever-silent spaces of the East,
Far-folded mists, and gleaming halls of morn.

Tithonus by Alfred, Lord Tennyson

For several years we've had the same little potted Christmas tree. I bring it indoors, nice and early, to acclimatize it before the kids decorate it for Christmas. I take a photograph of it – complete with home-made Angel Gabriel (who looks exactly like Alan Titchmarsh) on the top – and I might tweet it. Once Christmas is over, the tree goes out into the garden again, where it sits in a shady spot until the following Christmas. Every year it has looked a bit scrawnier, but never has it died. It is the Tithonus of Christmas trees – seeming to possess immortality, but not eternal youth, and no desire to grow or thrive.

I first saw this tree at Candy's Florist, opposite the Nail Bar. We were new to town, having literally moved house *that* day, and I thought a Christmas tree might perk us up. I parked across Candy's side alleyway, dashed into the shop and asked if they had any Christmas trees. Candy mentioned that I'd blocked her van in. I assumed that would be all right, seeing as she was there, in the shop, and I hadn't disappeared into the Nail Bar to have nativity scenes painted on to my fingernails. She didn't quite agree and described a hypothetical scenario in which she might need to race off in her van, and having to wait while I moved my Bongo making the difference between a life-and-death wreath delivery. I offered to move it and come back.

'No, leave it,' she said and pointed to a lopsided

little fir tree in a pot and told me it was the last one she'd got.

It looked half dead, but I examined it anyway — out of politeness.

Candy stood at the flower-arranging counter wrapping poinsettias in tinted cellophane and green ribbon. 'It's not a good specimen,' she said and suggested I try the out-of-town garden centre or Homebase or Sainsbury's or the Pannier Market.

I realized I didn't want to go anywhere else. I wanted to go home and unpack our belongings. 'This one should beef up, though, with a bit of TLC,' I said, 'shouldn't it?'

'No, it won't beef up, it should never have tried to make that size,' said Candy. 'It's been badly handled as a sapling and should've been thinned out of the plantation, like a radish, to help the healthier seedlings — now it's just a snag.'

'A *snag*?'

'Yeah,' said Candy, 'it's traumatized, probably been like that for years, but it's on its last legs now, it might freak if you take it indoors and fuck about with it.'

'What's a snag?'

'A standing, dead or dying tree, inactive equilibrium.'

I examined it again. I imagined it covered in baubles, etc. It didn't look that bad to me. Candy galloped her fingers on the desk and chewed a biro.

It had a good, angel-worthy top, but then nothing much in the middle, and most of the important lower branches were good for nothing – bald and gnarly, like broken fingers.

'You won't want it, it's not up to the job,' Candy said, looking up from her bouquet-wrapping jobs.

She was the wrong kind of person to disagree with – she had the strong opinions of someone with qualifications and experience. There was a framed certificate on the wall behind her. I daren't look at it – she was the sort to notice and make something of it or launch into a certificate-based anecdote. I knew it was hers, anyway, by her confident use of jargon.

In spite of Candy's well-qualified opinion, there was something about the little tree that appealed to me. I tried to explain it – half to myself, half to Candy.

'I'm not that bothered about bushiness, as such, I'm more interested in tallness,' I said. 'And because this tree is so scrawny, it looks tall – even though it's quite small,' I reasoned. 'And if we don't take it, who will?' I wondered.

'It's just a snag,' said Candy, squinting at me.

Candy really didn't want me to take the tree. I wondered briefly if there was a hidden agenda. Not that she looked like the sort to hide agendas.

'Do *you* want this tree?' I asked. 'Is *that* it?'

Candy laughed. Of course she didn't want it. She'd

chosen hers three weeks ago, pick of the crop, a perfectly symmetrical Fraser with silvery needles, so shiny, it looked fake, and the perfect shape for her narrow lounge-diner. She'd decorated it already with her granddaughter. I wanted to say she didn't look old enough to have a granddaughter, but you never know how that's going to go down these days.

'I think I'm going to take this tree,' I said, a little anxiously.

'You got kiddies at home?' asked Candy, menacingly.

'Yes, and they'll be delighted with it,' I said.

'No, they won't,' said Candy, 'kiddies hate trees like that, plus it might die on you — have you thought about how that's going to affect your Christmas?'

She was wrong. This tree needed a home and we needed a tree. My kids were still young. They told me I looked like a princess on the occasions I changed out of my pyjamas. They weren't going to see this tree as a 'snag', they'd love the idea of it being rescued, and they'd cover it with tinsel and adore it. Thinking this, I felt imbued.

I suddenly understood how my friend Stella must have felt when she first saw Sparky — the troubled collie-corgi cross — at the dog pound in Glasgow, when all around her the staff tried their utmost to persuade her against him. 'He's a collie,' they said, 'he'll need constant intellectual stimulation, you'll be forever hiding toy rabbits behind cushions for him to seek, and he'll get cleverer and cleverer until there are no hiding places left. And then he might *turn*.'

But Sparky seemed sweet, and his sad backstory (mistreated by a farmer with a mean streak) had captivated Stella. 'But look at his funny, pointy ears,' she said to the pound staff.

Still they tried to put her off with warnings about how he'd been traumatized as a pup – neglected and undernourished – and how he'd never make a family pet. Even if she subscribed to *Dog Puzzle Weekly* she'd never manage to keep his mind occupied long enough to prevent him chewing the table legs to dust, and weeing on the carpet out of boredom and post-traumatic stress.

I told Candy about Sparky. 'The dog pound advised her against him, said he was all wrong for her circumstances,' I said, 'but she put him in the back of her Ford Fiesta and took him home anyway.'

'Idiot,' said Candy.

I took the tree. Obviously.

At home I plonked the tree down on a low table.

'Is it meant to look like that?' asked a member of my family.

'Is that going to be our actual Christmas tree?' asked my daughter.

'It's been mistreated,' I said. 'It was meant to be a Christmas tree but hasn't had the chance. Let's give it one lovely Christmas covered in baubles and bells, and then let it fade away with dignity in the back garden.'

'I hate it,' said my daughter.

'Will we get a proper tree next year?' asked my son, a kinder person than my daughter.

'Yes,' I said.

But the tree never has faded away. It has lived.

It hasn't grown any bigger or bushier, and a few bits have broken away – as if it has some kind of deficiency, but I'm not sure what. At least three expert gardeners have examined it and all have advised the same thing: it needs to be kept out of bright sunlight and kept hydrated (don't we all?), and it'll go one way or the other. But it has neither died nor thrived, like a boutique on a high street – it has merely 'continued'.

I've repotted it, adjusted its position (shade, light sun, no sun, dappled sun). I've fed it (pine food) and not fed it. I stood it near an oak tree to give it big ideas and near some ugly bamboo to boost its esteem. I've pruned the dead 'branches' off and, a couple of years ago, it suddenly threw out a set of impressive pine cones at its crown. I assumed that was to be its swansong, but not so. Also, I've told and retold the story of how it was badly handled as a seed and sapling by a mean plantsman and never should have made it, etc.

This December, after years of service, I decided it was probably time we got a proper tree. Not that we were going to euthanize the snag, we were just getting it some help. Plus we were having people round.

I thought we'd go to Candy's but when I described to my daughter where Candy's was, she told me that Candy's had been a nail bar for the last five years at least. 'Another nail bar?' I cried.

'Yes, there are four now,' she told me.

We went to the out-of-town garden centre, where they'd transformed their patio and slabs area into a Christmas tree forest, thick with assorted pine trees in pots and in piles and hanging from makeshift rafters. Christmas music drifted and seasonal staff in elf costumes bobbed around and held up trees for customers, and measured and twirled them. It truly was like being in Narnia, albeit with loading pallets and price and info tags flapping in the breeze and the 'snow' just a roll of fluffy polyester with fag burns. But still, it was nice.

Suddenly, there stood Candy chewing a biro. She had changed a bit over the years; her hair colour was now bright green, whereas before it had been brown, and her name badge read 'Elf Helper' but I knew about fake names in retail. She seemed less authoritative but more approachable as an elf.

Candy asked if we'd like to complete the computerized Christmas Tree Audit. I said we definitely would. We crowded round a snow-topped computer and Elf Candy began tapping away at the keyboard and then explained that we were to highlight between three and six essential words from the list of TREE ATTRIBUTES and then up to three more from the CUSTOMER SPEC list and then click on the FIND MY TREE lozenge and the computer would tell us which tree we wanted.

Candy thrust the mouse at me. We gazed at the options.

TREE ATTRIBUTES
Piney-fragrance, fresh, pungent, mild, conical, slim, tall, symmetry, traditional, strong-of-branch, drooped, upward, dense foliage, sparse, medium, spruce, Norway spruce, noble fir, Nordmann fir, Fraser fir, Scots pine, indoor, outdoor, indoor/outdoor, roots, cut, log-mounted, bevelled, potted, stand-affixed, green, blue-green, silver-green, intense green, dark green, soft-needled, good retention, needle-sure, value, premium, luxury, dwarf, 2–3′, 3–4′, 4–5′, 5–6′, giant.

CUSTOMER SPEC

Children, babies, teenagers, elderly, allergies, dogs, cats, snakes, aquarium, cat-guarded, home delivery, refuse collection, hot, cold, unstable, dry, light, dark, electrical equipment, food prep, vulnerable surfaces, industrial, haz-chem.

I tentatively selected 'piney fragrance'. Candy agreed this was a good choice. 'Some aren't piney – some are a bit woody, smell-wise – and piney is more Christmassy.'

My daughter, being an artist, said, 'Conical'.

I clicked it.

Candy sighed. 'Everyone selects "conical",' she said. 'It's a total waste of a choice, they're all conical – it just means "cone-shaped".'

I made a sound of despair, but Candy seized the mouse and unselected 'conical'.

I asked Candy what she thought about 'green' as a choice, and winced.

'Yeah, "green" is an OK choice – if you want a green tree,' she said.

I clicked 'green'.

My son selected 'soft-needled' with our dog's paw pads in mind. I chose 'needle-sure' and my daughter chose 'symmetrical'. We had one left and we scanned the list. We froze, until I shouted, 'Oh my God, *potted*, I almost forgot, potted.'

'OK,' said Candy, 'now select three from the customer spec list and you're done.'

My daughter selected 'dogs', which no one could argue with. I chose 'children'. And my son selected 'snakes'. I was about to ask him to rethink but Candy looked so impressed I left it at that. And then, magically, the computer chose our tree.

After she had introduced us to our new tree, Candy suddenly seemed to remember me from before.

'How did your friend get on with that collie-cross?' she asked.

'Sparky,' I said. 'He's won endless rosettes for obedience and knows over fifty commands.'

'But he bites if you try to stroke him,' said my daughter.

'Only if you waggle your fingers in front of his face,' I said.

'And he chases cars. It's really dangerous,' said my son.

'Only red ones and tractors,' I said.

I heaved our five-foot high, snake-friendly Nordic fir with roots and a red plastic pot on to a flatbed trolley.

'And what happened to that snag I sold you, back a while?' asked Candy.

It was all coming back to her.

'Still going strong,' I said.

'She's chucked it out now,' said my daughter.

'I haven't *chucked it out*, I've retired it,' I said brightly. 'It's done us seven years.'

'Six,' said my daughter.

'Tsk!' tutted Candy. 'I told you it wouldn't last.'

THE CHRISTMAS LUNCH: A Story

The Christmas lunch party had been Bunny Wedgwood's idea. Emma had let herself be talked into it — she couldn't quite remember why. But then Bunny had pulled out the day before, having been sectioned by her daughter and son-in-law. Notification of this came from Bunny herself, apparently calling from a phone box in the cafeteria of Carlton Hayes Psychiatric Hospital on the outskirts of Leicester.

Bunny claimed to have been admitted 'just for Christmas and the worst of the winter' and expected to be home — albeit on tablets — by Shrove Tuesday.

'Philip Larkin's mother was here, in 1956. Just over

Christmas,' Bunny had boasted. 'She was quite mad, but set free again.'

The ridiculous lateness of Bunny's cancellation meant that Emma was stuck with giving a lunch to some dreadful people — Norah and Harry Hunter, and Babs and Frank Miller — and with no Bunny to act as a buffer.

On the day, with just over an hour before the guests were due to arrive, Emma noticed the label on the polythene bag of defrosting turkey casserole read 'blackberry & app'. She went to the deep freeze in the garage, and had a dig through the endless frosty little bags. Emma remembered she'd invited Babs without mentioning Frank. Partly because he was odious, and partly because catering for anything above five was a squash around the table. But Babs had assumed Frank was included anyway — the way couples did — and that was that.

She dug a bag of turkey casserole out of the depths, took it inside, thrust it into a pan of water and put it on a very low heat to defrost while she went to get herself ready. Bloody Frank Miller — she couldn't stand him.

Mid flannel wash, it suddenly occurred to Emma that Bunny might show up, after all, and this whole 'sectioned' thing might have been a joke — one never quite knew with Bunny. But thinking it through, she decided it probably wasn't a joke. She'd heard dreadful Christmas music and wailing in the background during the phone call.

Emma put on a beige, light wool dress and a dab of rouge and was about to walk through a haze of Chanel, when she noticed the awful stench – as if a laboratory had caught fire. One had, once – a lab, caught fire – in a village nearby, and the smell had hung in the air for days and made one feel anxious. Rushing through the hall, she knocked over a bowl of Christmas cranberry potpourri and, arriving at the stove, saw that somehow the casserole pan was on a high heat, the pan handle had melted away and the water had all evaporated, leaving the polythene bag to burn. She switched the gas off, opened a window and decided to concentrate on the chestnut soup starter.

The soup was thawed nicely in a Tupperware. *Carols from King's* played on the CD player and the fairy lights twinkled among some Christmas foliage in a copper pan. Emma transferred the jellified soup into a handsome orange saucepan and put it on a very low heat while she sliced a French stick. Then the phone rang. It was her daughter, Penny. She told Penny about Bunny Wedgwood's late cancellation. Penny immediately offered to make up the six.

'No,' Emma snapped. 'No, thank you.' She didn't want Penny showing up in one of her smocks and those ghastly earrings, hoovering up all the bread and asking for more butter and so forth.

To change the subject she told her about Bunny being sectioned by her son-in-law, which was a mistake, as Penny seemed terribly upset and wanted to dwell on it.

'Heavens! Poor Bunny,' said Penny. 'Do you think she's allowed visitors?'

Frankly, Emma resented Bunny getting all this attention — and skiving out of Christmas — when she was as sane as a spaniel. It was she, Emma, who could do with a bit of TLC in a secure place and having a year off. Now Penny was planning to dash off to Carlton Hayes with a literary magazine and a flask of mulled wine.

'No, no visitors, I shouldn't think,' said Emma.

'But it's Christmas,' whined Penny.

As Penny droned on about Bunny, Emma dipped her little finger into the orange saucepan and discovered it was coffee-flavoured ice cream, not chestnut soup. She hung up on Penny, chucked the pan into the sink, stomped out to the garage and went digging in the deep freeze again.

She flung things out so that she could rummage properly for the soup. Bags and tubs were strewn around; some landed on the woodpile, some on the roof of the car, and others just sat on the concrete floor. There was no soup in the freezer. She surveyed the jettisoned items and there, sitting on top of a can of creosote, was a tub with 'chest soup' scrawled across the lid. She kicked the can and the tub toppled off. She kicked the tub; it spun and crashed against the car tyre but remained intact. She should have picked it up and taken it inside and started heating it thoroughly – on a low heat. Instead, she took the wood-axe, smashed the tub and its frozen contents to bits and came out of the side door, rubbing her hands down her dress.

Inside, she made up two packets of Batchelors chicken and leek soup according to the instructions, with two pints of tap water.

Soon, the soup was boiling and the discs of prematurely sliced bread sat in a basket. Emma blew the dust off a tinselly centrepiece that Penny had made at a therapeutic craft class and popped it on the table with a candle stub. The smell of melted polythene and scorched lab rats was beginning to dissipate.

The doorbell rang.

Emma did a good job of greeting Norah and Harry – even though they were very rudely twenty minutes early – and gave them G&Ts from the drinks trolley in the sitting room. Norah presented Emma with a blousy poinsettia and questioned Emma about the oily handprints on the front of her dress – as if it was any of her concern.

'Oh, Emma,' she said, 'your lovely Jaeger. How did it happen? *Do* go and sponge it off before it marks.'

In the bathroom Emma dabbed at the dress with a sea sponge, and the image of Frank, years ago, in a

Christmas hat popped into her head and made her feel furious. She considered changing the dress, but the beige was her most flattering, and Harry and Norah had seen her in it now. Then she heard Frank's voice at the bathroom window, as if he was coming round the side of the house. Emma rushed into the sitting room to find him and Babs coming in through the French windows.

'We rang and rang,' Frank said, laughing. 'Babs thought we must've come on the wrong day.'

'I've snagged my tights on the blasted lavender,' wailed Babs.

Emma glanced down at the catastrophic ladders on Babs's cow-like legs and turned away so as not to have to look. She splashed G&T into glasses for them.

'Just tonic for Babs, she's under the doctor,' Frank boomed and guffawed.

Fetching more tonics, Emma glanced at herself in the hall mirror. She was red in the face and dishevelled but looked very slim indeed. Plonking the tonics on the trolley, she told the guests she'd be a minute fixing the meal and crunched through the potpourri to the kitchen-diner. The chicken and leek soup was raging. She was surprised – somehow, it was turned up high, when she thought she'd switched it off. She flung a tea towel over the spoiled casserole.

'Look,' she told herself, 'it's only the Millers and

the Hunters. The Frank thing was years ago, and the Hunters have got that strange son who lives in a car near the Baptist Church.'

She sprinkled some parsley flakes on to the soup and tried to think about the Hunters' boy again. Hadn't he changed his name to something odd – Gerontius or Grotius? Cheered by that, she decided she'd get the guests through to the table, serve the soup, tell them about Bunny being in the nuthouse and, while they discussed that and glugged wine, she could repair the main course.

'If you'd like to come through,' she said, ushering them towards the door.

But Harry continued with the end of a story and they all howled with laughter at it. It reminded Frank of a story of his own, and off he went. Frank's story, about two nuns in the bath, lasted forever, and eventually – before he'd got to the punchline – Emma interrupted.

'Please,' she said through gritted teeth, 'would you make your way to the table.' She followed it with a merry little laugh, but it came out wrong and Babs gave her a thunderous look.

Emma went back to the kitchen and slopped the scummy soup into rustic bowl-cum-mugs and set them on the table. They'd come from petrol coupons, but looked retro and fun. The guests trooped in and stood waiting for directions.

'Sit anywhere,' said Emma.

'Shouldn't we wait for Bunny?' asked Babs.

Emma ignored her.

But Babs persisted. 'Emma, are we expecting Bunny?'

'She's running late,' said Emma.

She couldn't be bothered to repeat the story Bunny had told her. The blazing Christmas tree, the accusations from the daughter, the son-in-law calling the doctor, the doctor calling a colleague, the shrieking and being held down in the back of the Volvo, etc, etc.

'Ooh, your lovely chicken soup again — delicious — we had this last time,' said Norah, curving her spoon into the soup.

Emma snatched it away. 'I'll get you something different.' She seized Harry's bowl, too, and slammed them both down on the draining board.

'Don't be ridiculous!' said Norah.

'No,' said Emma, 'you can't give people the same thing twice — it was the first thing I learned at Prue Leith.'

Emma rattled about in the fridge for a while and then plonked a tub of cottage cheese and chives down beside the breadbasket. 'There,' she said and, turning to Frank, barked, 'Have *you* had this soup before?'

'I don't think so,' said Frank.

'You?' she said, turning to Babs.

'Yes, it's Batchelors chicken and leek, we have it

every Saturday after golf,' said Babs wearily. 'Shall we just eat it?'

Emma shrugged and sat down next to Harry. The image of the wood-axe popped into her head.

Nip out and get it and tell this rabble to clear out, she thought. She looked straight ahead, trance-like.

'Nip out and get what?' Harry asked.

'Are you not eating?' Norah asked.

'No,' Emma replied vacantly, 'I don't want to get fat.' Emma was aware of an awkwardness and took a deep breath. 'The fat gene runs in the family. Mother was borderline obese,' she explained, 'and you've seen Penny – she's barely thirty and already beef to the heel.'

'I thought your mother suffered with agoraphobia,' said Babs, with a sniff.

'Precisely. She couldn't face anyone in that state,' said Emma, puffing out her cheeks to illustrate.

Frank sniggered.

Emma heard various whisperings, and became aware that she was resting her head on the tablecloth; she could feel the seersucker bumpy against her cheek. She was trying to remember the name of the Hunters' son. Something peculiar.

She may have fallen asleep for a moment or two, and she sat up with a start.

'Geronimo!' she said, and shot up to fetch the lemon meringue, which had hopefully reached room temperature by now. She placed it on the table and all four said how wonderful it looked.

'Aha! Lemon meringue, my favourite!' said Harry.

'Very Christmassy!' said Frank, with a wink.

'Coffee!' Emma shouted. 'Who wants coffee?' And she swung round to flick the switch on the ready-to-go percolator.

She fetched the coffee tray and spent a while looking in the fridge for a jug of cream. Then she cut the meringue, gave them a quarter each, and just as she passed Harry the fattest piece, the percolator stopped popping. 'Perfect timing,' she said and went to look for the cream in the garage.

Emma was still trying to recall the name of the Hunters' strange son – it can't have been Geronimo, that would be ridiculous – when suddenly the guests were gone. *That went well*, she thought.

She saw Harry had left his jacket on the back of his chair, then remembered Norah being miffed for some reason. (Had they been wearing the same dress?)

And she was puzzled to see the wood-axe embedded in the tinselly centrepiece.

FLAMING PUDDING

Every year, in early December, I send a Christmas pudding to my old friend Marie, who lives in France. I send it because Marie can't get it in the shops over there, and apparently loves it. This year, I found myself thinking I might switch to something else instead – say, a Christmassy book (the one you're reading now) – but I wondered about the etiquette of suddenly, without warning, breaking a Christmas tradition in this way.

I asked a well-behaved friend, 'Can I just stop sending Marie's Christmas pudding, or should I warn her?'

First the friend said, 'Can't you send the pudding *and* the book?'

And I said, of course I couldn't. Because that would be overgenerous, and overgenerosity is worse than meanness at Christmas and can be interpreted as 'needy' or passive-aggressive.

The friend conceded this but then asked why I would send an edible gift to someone who lived in the food capital of the world? 'Especially a Sainsbury's Basics microwavable Christmas pudding!'

'She really likes it,' I said, 'and it's Taste the Difference.'

'How do you know she likes it?'

'She says so.'

'Of course she does, she's being polite,' said my friend. 'She probably dies laughing at it every year.'

Until that moment, I'd been *certain* that Marie really loved Christmas pudding – and so did her partner and cat. I'd thought of myself as the saviour of their Christmas. Now I had visions of them all laughing and joking about it – in French.

And, thinking about it, I couldn't remember which had come first: her saying how much she liked Christmas pudding, or my sending it. I suddenly doubted myself and, feeling mortified about the fifteen or so puddings I've sent, emailed her.

Dearest Marie, I hope you won't be disappointed

but I'm considering not sending you a Christmas pudding this year. I might send you a book instead, because a) I think you'll love the book, and b) I suddenly wonder if you actually like Christmas pudding?

This all made me think long and hard about Christmas pudding. Partly because I think about Christmas a lot, and partly because I think about puddings a lot. And I came to the conclusion that *no one* likes Christmas pudding. Even the one person I know categorically to like it (Granny Kate) takes the whole of the Christmas period to finish a tiny pudding that's meant for one person (whereas with any other type of pudding – say, treacle or jam – she'd be finished in one go, scraping the bowl with her spoon and wishing there were seconds) and I think that counts as not really liking it, as such.

As a child I used to accept a portion of pudding, but only because it had five-pence pieces hidden inside, and I never ate it. Once I'd checked it for cash, I'd spoon it into the dish of the person sitting next to me while they gazed out of the window looking for the robin I'd seen hopping about on an upturned wheelbarrow. My sister used to pretend to like it too, but she was just showing off and trying to appear grown up and has since admitted hating it. One year, in the late 1970s, we were served Christmas Pudding

Parfait (a kind of coinless Christmas pudding/ice cream hybrid invented by Marguerite Patten or Mary Berry). This caused an outcry, and the truth — that we resented Christmas pudding ruining our ice cream, because we all hated it — came out. This confession was followed by intense guilt and regret at the idea that we had possibly consigned Christmas pudding to oblivion as far as our family was concerned. But not so. A small, flaming thing appeared the following year and we all dug for coins and smeared it around a plate as if nothing had been said.

So, given all this, what is the likelihood of Marie and her French partner and cat actually liking it?

I'm not saying people don't *like* Christmas pudding per se; they just don't like *eating it*. They definitely like it — but for other reasons. *I* like it. I actually *love* it — the idea of it. Its Christmassy-ness, the smell of it, the money in it. I even quite like watching Granny Kate cover her tiny portion in brandy-flavoured, non-dairy, sugar-free condiment, and spread it around the dish and pretend to have relished it. I love its roundness. Its cartoon depiction (dome-shaped, with white icing and holly) is truly one of the nicest, most delightful images of Christmas. One year, somebody clever gave Granny Kate some Christmas pudding earrings, and none of us could stop looking at them and smiling as they dangled under her white bob.

My sister used to have an illustration in her kitchen of nervous-faced, red-cheeked Mrs Cratchit bringing the pudding to the Cratchit family Christmas table, with an excerpt in festive copperplate on a facing page:

In half a minute Mrs Cratchit entered: flushed, but smiling proudly: with the pudding, like a speckled cannon-ball, so hard and firm, blazing in half of half-a-quartern of ignited brandy, and bedight with Christmas holly stuck into the top.

Oh, a wonderful pudding! Bob Cratchit said, and calmly too, that he regarded it as the greatest success achieved by Mrs Cratchit since their marriage. Mrs Cratchit said that now the weight was off her mind, she would confess she had had her doubts about the quantity of flour. Everybody had something to say about it, but nobody said or thought it was at all a small pudding for a large family. It would have been flat heresy to do so. Any Cratchit would have blushed to hint at such a thing.

OK, so the Cratchit family liked eating the pudding. But, to be fair, they were almost starving – plus they literally lived in Dickensian times, before we had chocolate yule logs or Viennetta.

The real reason people continue to *believe* they

like Christmas pudding is the excitement of setting fire to it. In the 1960s and 70s, when I was a child, causing a house fire with a blazing food item was a common occurrence because of all the Crêpes Suzette, flambéed bananas, flaming toddies – and especially the chip pans, which constantly caught fire and had to be smothered with a damp tea towel. We even had a tea towel printed with the instructions for putting out a pan fire. I particularly remember the instruction: *When flames have died down, if possible, move the pan out of the house, walking backwards to avoid the hot oil spilling.* To be honest, we all dreaded having to deal with the chip pan fire, because of the need to walk backwards out of the house with the hot oil, whereas out-of-control Christmas puddings were deemed less of a problem and were often less strictly monitored.

Because of the excited state of the molecules, Christmas pudding flames are blue and, therefore, not quite as visible as the bright yellow ones and can creep along the table unnoticed and jump from Orla Kiely napkin to Orla Kiely napkin to origami nativity centrepiece and then, before you know it, the tablecloth has caught and the pile of cracker debris and discarded wrapping paper is ablaze and everyone is falling drunkenly over each other trying to run away or switch the lights on. Nowadays someone will film the whole thing on their phone – and, this way, people are held to account afterwards. If you have said, 'You fucking idiot, Dad,' or trampled your young niece in order to save yourself, or rushed in from the garage with a mini fire extinguisher, realized you've over-reacted, and flung it into the arms of an elderly relative, there's no denying it, it's all there on film.

And, like footage of badly driven cars and the film my son made of my friend Stella and me being repeatedly knocked over by waves off the coast of Fal-mouth, the chaos of the pudding emergency always makes great watching and balances the dullness of the turkey main course. In fact, I'm now wondering if my personal enjoyment of a pudding fire is simply a response to my fear and loathing of turkey – the small mealtime devastation offering a kind of redress? I don't know.

I have heard of many Christmas pudding fire stor-ies. The neighbour who smothered their raging pudding with a daughter's brand-new Christmas present coat. The friend whose mother actually had to call the fire brigade and evacuate the house because the fire took hold and consumed the entire kitchen. And the neighbour who threw the flaming pudding out of a window and set fire to the shed. But no Christmas fire has ever been as pleasing as the one I witnessed, in a Leicestershire pub, many years ago with an elderly relative who was being a tiny bit impatient with the beleaguered waiting staff.

After a slightly fraught main course (the elderly relative having complained that the turkey was 'very dry'), her portion of traditional pudding arrived but it wasn't on fire.

'Young man,' the relative said to the waiter, 'I want my pudding *alight.*' And she handed the dish back to him.

'*Alight?*' asked the waiter, not familiar with the tradition.

'Yes, yes, you know, flames, alight.' And she gestured to the little flame on the candle in our Christmas table centrepiece.

When the waiter brought the pudding back, it had a great candle stuck into it and he began to click his lighter.

'No,' said the elderly relative, 'alight, with brandy – brandy.' Pointing to the bar, she repeated, loudly, 'Brandy!'

The waiter returned with a glass of brandy and the relative took matters into her own hands. She tipped the brandy over the pudding and, after a few false starts with the waiter's Bic lighter, it suddenly whooshed and went up in a liquid blue fireball, catching her paper hat and napkin in a second.

The astonished waiter, quick as a flash, seized the water jug, flung it over her and the pudding, walked away and came back with a small towel.

Sadly, this was before people filmed everything.

Postscript: I had a short reply from Marie regarding Christmas pudding.

Bonjour!
Book would be lovely. But can't say we wouldn't miss your hilarious little Xmas puds!

I'm taking this as a plea for a continuation of the puddings, so I shall send her one, as usual, and will get my mother to tag her in a Facebook post about the book. Then it's up to her.

TIMOTHY THE CHRISTMAS TURKEY: A Story

It was still summer when my dad sent the first email on the subject of our next family Christmas, and it had an attachment.

Dear Daughters.

You'll be delighted to hear that I discovered Damson Tree Farm, a high-welfare turkey farm, quite near us and have ordered an organic heritage bird expected to achieve a weight of between

15 and 20 lbs in time for Xmas lunch. Your mother will provide the usual trimmings. Dx

Attached was a photograph of a fluffy object — apparently an eight-week-old turkey poult, called Timothy.

The thing was, the previous Christmas, as we'd sat down to lunch, my older sister had enquired about the welfare status of the turkey we were about to eat.

'Is it organic free range?' she'd asked.

Our mother, who'd bought it as a frozen item from a supermarket, couldn't say for sure.

My sister then said she'd rather eat a turkey that had had a happy life scratching about with its flock siblings. My other sister and I totally agreed. It put a bit of a downer on Xmas lunch, to be honest, thinking of the bird stuck in a hutch and drip-fed antibiotics.

Dad's next Christmas email came quite soon after the first.

Dear Daughters.
Timothy is doing well. He's moved on to adult food after the starter crumbs and, though on the small side, the farmer says he'll easily fill out to the target 18 lbs by Xmas. Dx

And there, in the attached photograph, was a dear little baby turkey. In the first picture he'd been a blur of yellowish fluff and might have been a rag from the sewing box. In this second picture, though, he looked cartoony with curious little eyes, a wonky beak and a bright yellow anklet. He was most definitely a bird of some sort. Definitely outside and not in a hutch.

I 'replied all' saying Timothy looked adorable and happy. I pressed 'send' too soon and regretted saying adorable.

The next email came in early autumn, when I was on my way to a team-building trip with the whole of the marketing department. I was surprised to see that Timothy now had the beginnings of the dangly throat thing and some impressive feather markings. And he looked so grown up.

Dear Daughters.
Jim and Gail (at Damson Tree) estimate that Tim will make 16–17 lbs by early December. He's very happy and particularly likes to have a chat with Gail when she feeds the flock after the school run. Dx

I forwarded the email to a couple of colleagues. They were most impressed by Timothy.

The next email on the subject was to Dad from my older sister, asking to be excluded from the Timothy updates. My younger sister and I were copied in.

> Dad.
> I do not wish to see pictures of our Xmas lunch while he's still alive. J.

I literally couldn't believe the October email. The picture showed a great plasticky turkey head and actually looked like something off *Doctor Who* and nothing at all like Tim. I replied.

> Dad, please don't zoom in so close to Tim. Also, are you sure it's actually Tim and not some random turkey? I'm remembering the time you took us to see Dolly the Sheep and it turned out not to be Dolly. Gx

I was at home for a weekend in October and got to actually meet Tim in the flesh when Dad and I went to Damson Tree Farm on the Sunday morning (visitor hours: 10.00–11.30).

Gail took us to the enclosure and told me not to touch the electric wire unless I had rubber gloves on (which, of course, I didn't). She scattered some damsons from a bucket and the flock crowded around her, gobbling and gurgling loudly.

'Timothy's wearing a bright yellow anklet,' said my dad, 'he's one of the smaller birds.'

Eventually, I spotted the bright yellow anklet. Tim was indeed a bit smaller than his flock siblings, who seemed to continually barge into him as they tried to peck at the fruit. Gail came out and explained that Tim was a slow grower but assured us he'd easily reach 15 lbs by December.

The next email included a less zoomed-in picture that I'd taken, showing Tim's relative smallness.

Dear Daughters.
Gail agrees that Tim's a tad smaller than ex-pected at this stage but this is typical of a polite little turkey like him (always last to the lunch bucket). This should sort itself out soon, though, and he should achieve 14–15 lbs by Christmas.

The email in late November showed Tim looking considerably bigger. He compared well, size-wise, against two other birds in the picture and was look-ing quite handsome.

Dear Daughters.
This will be my last Tim update. He's almost 12 lbs now and still 3 weeks to go until 13th December (slaughter). I shall collect him on the 23rd. Dx

I felt tearful and rang my mum. She said I was being silly, which I was. I put Tim out of my mind and concentrated on the Christmas direct mail campaign I was working on.

The next email on the subject of Christmas was from my younger sister saying she couldn't face going home for Christmas on account of Tim. And then, my older sister emailed to say she'd spend the day with my younger sister – also to avoid Tim.

Dad replied saying that, bearing everything in mind, he and Mum had decided to forego the £40 deposit they'd paid for Tim and that, instead, our mother would fetch an anonymous capon from the village butcher and offer a veggie alternative. My sisters replied saying, in that case, they'd come home as planned and asking what would happen to Tim (and what a capon actually was).

My dad replied that a capon was a happy rooster that had been castrated at a young age, making its meat more tender and less gamy. And that Tim – due to being undersized – would probably become a family pet at Damson Tree Farm, at least until next year.

The journey home on the evening of the 23rd in my older sister's Polo was long and the traffic was bad. And though we dreaded having to see the anonymous capon all plucked, stuffed and basted, we agreed that at least it wouldn't be Tim – and even if someone else *would* be eating him, it wouldn't be this year and it wouldn't be us.

On Christmas Eve, I caught sight of the capon sitting in the baking tin surrounded by chunks of onion, peppercorns and bay leaves. While I gazed at it, having a few thoughts, my mother grabbed its feet and began forcing handfuls of Delia's grape stuffing into its cavities. Then, noticing me there, she stopped what she was doing and turned to empty the chopping board into the food recycling bin: onion skins, orange peel, parsley stalks – and a bright yellow thing.

'Mum!' I gasped.

'Make some coffee and keep your mouth shut,' she said.

CHRISTMAS CORRESPONDENCE

The letters to Santa

Children don't seem to write many letters to Father Christmas nowadays. They stop believing in him by the age of eight – unlike my generation, who remained loyal until we left home. Writing to him was a big deal. We wrote from home and school, and sometimes privately, and posted our letters into the snow-capped postboxes that popped up all over the place, and specially recruited elves would take them by the sackful to Greenland or Lapland – or wherever he lived back then.

Although I was a keen letter writer, I never felt

comfortable writing to Father Christmas. I didn't like explaining myself, and hated the begging aspect. I didn't trust an elf to deliver my letter and, even if one did, I didn't believe Father Christmas would have time to read it. Not only that, I had concerns about privacy. There were various other people who might sneakily read it – people who had a vested interest. A parent, a sibling, some mischievous elves, maybe even Mrs Christmas – who knew?

At school, I resented the way Christmas expectation was dangled in front of us and exploited and our efforts scrutinized and used against us by teachers, who – far from wanting to enhance Christmas – were only interested in catching us out being greedy, or presumptuous, or thoughtless, or bad at spelling Christmas, or missing the 'e' in grateful or just not seeming grateful enough. I was a perfectly good speller at that time, but having my decency assessed was always a worry. It wasn't as if we even wanted to write to Father Christmas. We didn't. We were constantly egged on by all the adults around us – and kids on telly – to go for the high-value presents, and we were conned into thinking this was the way.

Letters to Father Christmas brought out a treacherous side to people, too – me included. I remember telling him – in one of many compulsory letters – that my sister Vic had stopped believing in God. I was hinting that she'd stopped believing in *him*, actually. I was too polite to come straight out with it but wanted to alert him as to her general scepticism. 'PS: I've *not* stopped believing in God. That's my sister, Victoria, who lives at the same address as me.'

Luckily for today's kids, they can text him or Snapchat him – or just ignore him – and they still get much better gifts than we ever did.

The thank-you letter

Thank-you letters are another Christmas nightmare. In my day a letter, written on writing paper, was required. I wrote them because I had to, and because forcing us to write detailed thank-you letters was my mother's most important Christmas tradition (except cooking a turkey).

I particularly hated them because they were a much bigger deal for me than for my siblings. For a start, I was a known letter-writer, and people had high expectations, plus I had double the amount of godparents. I had the usual nearby uncle who did no harm, a Canadian theatre agent who had an actor boyfriend called Alan (but not Bates) who my parents had palled up with in their London days. And a posh second cousin of my mother's who'd been recruited because she was nice and had a farm. All very much the norm. But then, I also had two extra, bogus ones – a Dutch businesswoman and her husband (I'm calling them Beatrix and Piet) who'd been accidentally asked by my mother when she couldn't think of anything to say at a business dinner and had just had a baby (me). They didn't show up at my christening and so my mother thought they'd forgotten all about it. But they hadn't, and they kept me going in Dutch comic books throughout my childhood and beyond.

My mother was a stickler. We weren't allowed to get away with scribbling 'Thank you for the present, love Nina' on a preprinted thank-you card. Her formula was as follows:

Dear Person = *Beatrix and Piet.*
Christmas wish = *Hope you had a nice Christmas.*
Health enquiry = *I hope you are well.*
Specific thanks = *Thank you for sending another*
Marten Toonder book. I have started to read it
already and it's very interesting.
Interesting comment = *So sorry that West Ger-*
many beat you 2-1 in the World Cup Final.
Kind sign off = *Lots of love, Nina.*
Quirky postscript = *PS Mum is pregnant.*

Children of my generation knew the importance of the Christmas thank you. It wasn't like the birthday thank you (the absence of which was far less noticeable due to it being any old time and no one's really looking). We were told that if we didn't send a proper, well-written thank-you letter by early January, the giver could legitimately never send another gift. If we said we didn't care, we'd take the risk, because actually we wouldn't mind not getting another gift from these people, the other, more serious, real reason for the letter would be invoked – i.e. if we didn't write a nice thank-you letter, the giver might slag my mother off terribly around the family and say what a menace she was. We knew this to be true because we'd heard my mother doing exactly this when she didn't receive nice thank yous from her nieces and nephews.

'I sent Polly a five-pound Body Shop voucher and I haven't heard a thing,' she might say, and then, 'I'll just give Marian a ring to check it got to her.'

And then we'd hear, 'No, no, not at all, please don't worry, I just wanted to make sure she'd actually received it – you know what the postal service can be like.'

And then, a few days later, she'd receive her thank-you letter: *Dear Auntie. I hope you are well. Etc.*

Soon after this, in retaliation, Auntie Marian might phone back to ask whether my brother had received the book *DIY Home Insulation* they'd sent him – only they'd not heard from him. And then my mother would be straight on the phone (to me).

'Did Jeremy ever write and thank Uncle Clive and Auntie Marian for that ludicrous book?' she might typically say.

'How should I know?'

'Marian says they've not heard from him.'

'It's not your problem,' I might say, 'He's forty-seven years old and a high court judge!'

'I know, but you don't understand,' she might say, 'it'll come back on me.'

When our much younger brother, Johnny, arrived in the world, my mother hadn't the stomach for a whole rerun of the thank-you letter stress, and so the minute he reached letter-writing age (six), she simply wrote every one of his thank yous for him and had them done and posted by December 27th. No arguments and no stress, no passive-aggression, no gossip about his literacy skills, no questions about her parenting or the poor beleaguered postal service.

This seemed the perfect solution, except that on his twenty-first birthday – after a meal at a restaurant on the Oadby bypass – Johnny opened a parcel from his godmother, Auntie Harriet, and out fell a bundle of old letters. It took us a while to understand that they were every single thank-you letter she'd received from him. Much debate afterwards as to whether this had been a really clever idea/innocent fun or an incredible act of forward-planning and vindictiveness.

Suffice to say, Johnny was delighted. My mother, not so much.

Receiving Christmas thank-you letters can be a bit gruelling, too. I can't help feeling that the main point of Christmas thank yous in January is to showcase the parenting. It might just be me, but they sometimes feel like a rebuke for not having forced my kids to write more consistently, on paper, in ink, and during the first quarter of the year.

Having said that, one of the nicest thank-you letters I ever saw was written by my own little son, aged seven.

Dear Mary-Kay,
Thank you for the helicopter. I like it.
You sent me one exactly the same last year but it's OK because that one smashed into a lamp and broke (so did the lamp).
I wasn't good at controlling helicopters then, but I am now.
Love from,
Alfred

Overall, though, I'd rather get a flippant and badly written text message in February and be able to slag the parent off.

The round robin

My mother doesn't send Christmas cards any more, except to her favourite cousin, and one or two dear, old friends – and she doesn't receive any back, except from the cousin.

'No one really bothers with cards any more,' she says. 'I do a Christmas message to my followers on Facebook.'

'What about the people who don't follow you on Facebook?' I say. 'Like me.'

'Tough luck,' she says.

And actually, I agree. I'm quite happy about the demise of the Christmas card but I do miss the Christmas round robin, which has also ceased to be. Round robins used to be how we found out how brilliantly our cousins and second cousins had done in their tests and exams or sports tournaments, and what their parents had been to see at Stratford. Nowadays I have to ask my mother for this type of news because she is on Facebook the whole time, sending and receiving informative, supportive and jolly messages.

'What's new?' I always ask her as we settle in John Lewis café for our tea and she looks straight at her phone.

Mother: Erm, I think Susan's car has failed its MOT.

Me: What makes you think that?

Mother: She's posted a picture of it, with a sad face emoji, look, I've liked it.

Me: Oh.

Mother: (*Still looking at phone*) Oh dear!

Me: What?

Mother: I think the bloke she was about to move in with has gone back to his ex.

Me: God, has she written that on Facebook?

Mother: No, but she's deleted photographs with him in and she's not following him any more. And if you click through to him ... look, that's his ex he's standing with. They're at a stock car race. I'm going to unfollow him.

To be honest, these bits of news wouldn't have actually made it into a round robin — too dull and vague and changeable. And that's my point: unlike Facebook, you knew where you were with a round robin. It was one or two A4 pages of solid news. There was a tacit round robin code of conduct, which stopped any nonsense. Plus they were only once a year and never interfered with your tea.

1. Inclusive

Your round robin had to be enclosed inside *each and every one* of your Christmas cards. Otherwise a two-tier system emerged and people could feel left out and unloved. This rule meant that my black-sheep-of-the-family mother received quite a few round robins from people who had dropped her in real life, or vice versa, and this was quite entertaining and gave my siblings and me a little peep into our wider family's lives.

2. Positive

If there was bad news, you had to show pluck by ending on a high:

> We moved house, had twins, Jim met someone else and we got divorced. On the plus side, I won a lifetime's supply of Paxo in a competition. Please note my new address.

3. No oversharing

People didn't feel the need to write the actual *facts*. No one wrote:

> We missed the ceremony because one of my daughters threw my bottle of whisky out of the car window on the M1 and the police pulled us over and breathalysed me.

They wrote instead:

> Everyone agrees that Hamish and Bina had a wonderful wedding.

4. No being overly modest

Self-deprecation didn't come into fashion until later. Round robins were allowed to be cram-packed with admirable works and liberal good deeds. Like the one from Georgina and Mike, which told of their almost single-handed crusade to wrestle a footpath from a greedy farmer who had been aggressively letting it become overgrown and kept blocking gate access with his tractor and an assortment of bladed machines.

Georgina (or Mike) were fully entitled to write:

A bare-chested Mike went berserk with a machete and – hey-presto – the footpath was soon navigable. He's now a hero in the village!

5. Informative

People sometimes took a didactic tone, but this wasn't a problem – and you could learn a lot.

Built new kitchen extension using sustainable glass bricks and planted cutting-edge ivy/wheat hybrid, to provide insulation and absorb pollutants.

Had marvellous holiday in Sri Lanka (known here as 'Ceylon' until 1972), a beautiful country with good railway infrastructure.

6. CV-like

Round robins, when hurriedly compiled, might read like the 'Personal Interests' section of a CV. But there was nothing wrong with that – especially when they revealed an aunt's love of weightlifting or an uncle's incompatibility with Sagittarians and love of barn dances.

7. Philosophical/Christmassy

Some round robins really got you in the Christmas mood, reminding you of goodwill to all men, etc. Others hit a slightly wrong tone and put a downer on things, like the one from our ex-piano teacher.

> John and I are not having Christmas this year. The world is just too fucking awful and unfair and we don't see anything to celebrate.

8. No trying to be funny

Trying to be funny in a round robin cancelled out the innate funniness. They were unintentionally funny. Spoofs were unpopular, unsporting and un-Christmassy.

9. Inventive styles

Some writers in my particular group used to occasionally experiment with different styles and layouts. I remember a stream-of-consciousness round robin from an old uncle, and still have a copy of my father and stepmother's 1999 offering, which featured the two of them faux-bickering about what they might include – it having been such an eventful year. It was written entirely in dialogue and went something like this:

Dad: You were ordained into the Church, weren't you, darling? I suppose we must mention that.

Stepmother: Yes, we should – as long as you don't blurt out that you're an ATHEIST.

Dad: Oh, all right.

10. Balance

Although boasting was very much permitted, it wasn't the done thing to present *only* your best news. This balancing was important if you wanted respect in your circle of family and friends and among the wider robining community. For every bronze medal there should really be an ingrowing toenail.

Below is a table to help illustrate this. The idea being that for every item mentioned from column A you had to include an item from column B.

Column A	Column B
New dog	Had to attend a wedding
New spaniel pup	Sued for whiplash
Pottery classes	Identity theft
Holiday	Car prang
Foreign holiday	Caught parking on a zigzag

Spanish holiday	Long weekend at Center Parcs
Baby	Cautioned for shouting at child's sport event
Twins	Tree fell on shed
First grandchild	Mudslide on branch line, chaos for months
Second grandchild	Wrongly incriminated in charity fraud
Ken Dodd in Newtown	*As You Like It* at Stratford upon Avon
Saudi business trip	Tests for allergies
Exam success	Lost luggage on Saudi business trip
Job promotion	Tesco Metro opens
Met Una Stubbs	Caught smoking on Google Earth
Mentioned in birthday honours	Had to attend another wedding
Built ha-ha wall that affords terrific views	Water contamination scare
Book deal	Allergy to red peppers
Ordained into the Church	Garden bonfire got out of hand
New home	Clay soil/rampant bamboo
New countryside home	Favourite brand of deodorant discontinued
Referenced in a scientific paper	Car vandalized in Stratford upon Avon
Ran a half-marathon	Jilted at the altar

Ran a marathon	Bankruptcy
Met Lenny Henry	Varicose veins
Joined dog-walking group	Awful weather on honeymoon
Waitrose opened a branch nearby	Bunion surgery
Christening	Trial separation
Nephew's BAFTA nomination	Appeared as a character in ex-lover's play
Daughter cast as Helen of Troy in play	Son cast as shepherd
Created drought-proof garden	Parked on neighbour's hosepipe

11. Anticipation

The round robin was the sitcom you never planned to watch – you'd heard of the characters, but didn't really watch the show. But now, after reading of your mother's second cousin's daughter's pole vault victory (second place), a connection was made that couldn't easily be broken and you longed for next year's instalment. And, like a sitcom, you never knew what might happen next: first place? School dropout? Switch to long jump? Run over by a tram?

Even a close relative – whom you thought you knew everything about – might reveal something interesting:

We've had a new fence (pre-creosoted).

Or surprising:

In February, Bill started a beard and, by June, was regularly being mistaken for Acker Bilk.

Or delightful:

We sold one of the retriever pups to Sting and Trudie – and have become quite pally since.

AN ALMOST COMPREHENSIVE GLOSSARY OF CHRISTMAS

A

Advent calendar: Should be a visual thing or a candle. Chocolate doesn't belong here. See *precedent setting*.

Amazon: Easy and seemingly convenient, but beware – wrapping paper is joyless, plain navy blue, plus all that cardboard. And having to answer the door is a pain and neither convenient nor Christmassy. See *bookshops*.

'Away in a Manger': Vic's favourite carol on account of 'cattle lowing'. Nostalgic, nice imagery, but turns needy at the end. Include on Christmas *playlist*.

B

Blood pressure kit: Not Christmassy. More suitable as a birthday gift, see *lawnmower* and *Hoover*.

Bookshops: Very Christmassy indeed, especially my local Waterstones where you can enjoy a gingerbread muffin or traditional Christmas dinner panini while you flick through your prospective gifts and watch people in the street below going about their Christmas business. See *napkins*.

Bread sauce: See *home-made food*.

Raymond Briggs: See *The Snowman*.

Brussels sprouts: Never call them 'Brussels'. Ignore Nigel Slater, just boil, do not roast or fry or add anything. You've got enough to do.

C

Central heating: Turn it down, there's nothing worse than a hot house when you're all togged up in Christmas-themed winter wear. See *elf costume*, *needle drop* and Christmas *jumper*.

Centrepiece: Festive foliage and a candle poked into a block of oasis. *Granny Kate*'s home-made centrepiece travels with her on Christmas visits and has only once been rejected.

Charity gifts: Be sure recipients aren't expecting a real flock of chickens and rudimentary henhouse. Also, as with real gifts, baby goats are more Christmassy than schoolbooks or bicycles. See *goats*.

Chocolate: See *Quality Street*.

Christmas: Also known as *Xmas*.

A *Christmas Carol*: By Charles Dickens. Book, films, Muppets – all good Christmas enhancers.

Christmas crackers: Don't read the statistics about how many crackers the world gets through every year.

Christmas Eve: The nicest bit of the festive season, in my opinion.

Christmas haters: Hating Christmas can be a cry for help.

Christmas lovers: People who 'love Christmas' can *turn* if things don't go to plan. See *Vic* and *Christmas haters*.

Christmas you never had: Try not to keep telling children you're giving them the Christmas you never had. Un-Christmassy.

Christmastime: American for *Christmas*.

Church: A bit like *The Vicar of Dibley* Christmas special, but longer.

Cranberry sauce: Putting *bread sauce* out of business.

Crime: See *wreath*.

Cunt-face: See *gift tags*.

D

Defrosting: See *illness*.

Delia: Smith, Christmassy, very good if you want *stuffing*.

Disco Deathbeat: Second-hand paperback porn-thriller given to my mother in 1995. See *funny gifts*.

Dogs: Not just for Christmas, plus beware Christmas food hazards. Good for social media.

Donkey: Apparently not in the Bible but who's to say a donkey didn't just wander in? See *purists*.

Drink: Champagne is nice on the day, but *Glue Vine* scents the home.

Dryness: See *Turkey*.

E

Eggnog: Chilled American beverage – traditionally made with milk, cream, sugar and whisked eggs. Mix with lemonade to produce the disgusting British drink *Snowball*.

Elf costume: Your employer might expect you to wear an elf costume throughout the Christmas period – especially if you work in a *toyshop*. Great if you suit green and like stripy tights, which I do. See also *SantaLand Diaries*.

Epiphany: The twelfth day of Christmas and the manifestation of Christ to the Gentiles as represented by the Magi. See *Twelfth Night*.

F

Fairy lights: Fast-twinkle mode, much favoured by

Vic, can be distracting and cause migraines. See *illness*.

U. A. Fanthorpe: Her Christmas poems are bliss, available.

Father Christmas: Leave him a *mince pie* and a *Snowball*, but don't start leaving fake, glittery Santa footprints. See *precedent setting* and *Santa Claus*.

Festivus: Secular, generic festival invented by the father of the inventor of George Costanza's father.

Fights: Most common after too much *Glue Vine*, playing *games*, arguing over the *wishbone*, or seeing someone with superior *charity gifts*. It's hard to stop people fighting, but you might try my mother's trick of announcing that she's been diagnosed with a serious *illness*.

Ella Fitzgerald: Include various on your *playlist* – but not one after the other, or your house will feel like a Jamie's Italian.

Food: When it's decided who's going to cook the actual meal, treat the person like a demigod. Let them choose the telly and the music and let them pull the *wishbone*.

Funny gifts: Wonderful when they work (see *German shepherd*), but beware; they don't always go down as well as you were hoping. See *Disco Deathbeat*.

G

Games: Can be fun but very often cause *fights* when

coupled with Christmas imprisonment. Best for not causing fights are Guess Who? and Boggle. Never risk Risk! or Monopoly, as these call up evil in even the meekest.

German shepherd: Portraits of big dogs make great *funny gifts.*

Gift tags: Clearly label your gifts to avoid wrongful distribution. See *cunt-face* and *One-at-a-Time Present Opening (OTPO).*

Gifts: The only excuse for not making a huge effort is that you're in hospital, prison, or have just had twins.

Gingerbread house: Flat-packed from *Lakeland* unless you've splashed out in IKEA, in which case count yourselves lucky. Seemingly Christmassy, but actually not. Especially if the children involved haven't heard of Hansel and Gretel.

Glue Vine: Proper pronunciation for Glühwein. See *mulled wine.*

Goats: the most enjoyable of the *charity gifts.*

Godparents: Choice of godparent is an indication of how much your parents liked you at birth. Your brother's: a wealthy, elderly relative with no offspring and a fatal condition. Yours: a robust young aunt who loves weaving. See *home-made gifts.*

Granny Kate: Christmas enthusiast and traditionalist. Enforcer of the Christmas *centrepiece*, hair brushing and using best china.

H

Handkerchief: Needed for wiping away Christmas tears, usually brought on by *Raymond Briggs*.

Happy Christmas: Better to wish someone 'a *Merry* Christmas' (even though it sounds a bit twattish), otherwise it's hard to also wish them 'a Happy New Year' without saying 'happy' twice.

Hawkin's Bazaar: Novelty gift and toy shop, offering a range of unusual toys, gifts, gadgets and curiosities that will appeal to many ages and tastes [**advertisement**].

Heroes: Mini replicas of ordinary chocolate bars that we all have twice a day, not Christmassy. See *Quality Street*.

Highlighter pens: See *Radio Times*.

Ho, Ho, Ho!: Only TV/film Father Christmases say this.

Noddy Holder: Composer (with Jim Lea) of the best Christmas song ever written.

Holly: Christmassy and real. Strew it around.

Home-made food: It's win-win these days. Do it all from scratch and get the plaudits, or buy it all from Iceland and look badass. Apart from *bread sauce*, which must be home-made.

Home-made gifts: Never that nice, unless you're a good marmalader or Grayson Perry, tbh.

Hoover: Never buy someone this for Christmas. See *lawnmower.*

Hyacinth bulb: Perfect teacher gift, both schooly and Christmassy.

I

Illness: Insufficiently thawed, undercooked and over-dry poultry can cause illness. Feigning sudden or serious illness or choking can stop *fights*. See *fairy lights*.

J

Jesus: The birth, and subsequent goodness of, being the original *true meaning*.

Jumper: Christmas clothing of any kind is much admired. Reindeer *onesie*, Christmas pudding earrings, pine-green nail varnish. The wearing of these is safer than the giving of. See *elf costume* and *central heating*.

K

Kids: See *onesie*.

Killjoys: The Christmas killjoy just needs lots of love and attention. See also *purists*, *Christmas lovers*.

The King's Speech: At the time of writing this is a film starring Colin Firth, but one day it will be instead of the Queen's Speech. We dread the day.

L

L-tryptophan: An amino acid occurring in *turkey*.

Some claim it causes drowsiness and will help you sleep right through the *OTPO* and the *Queen's Speech*.

Lakeland: Budget homewares retailer, with a branch in Truro but not Leicester (true reason for Vic's early December visit). See *Vic*.

Lawnmower: Never get anyone this for Christmas. See *Hoover* and *blood pressure kit*.

Leicester: Excellent for Christmas shopping, but no *Lakeland*.

M

Meltis New Berry Fruits: Loved by Jessie Stibbe, my paternal granny, and therefore loved by me, though not to eat.

Merry Christmas: Preferable to *Happy Christmas*. Especially popular in the USA.

Mince pies: Roughed-up shop ones look home-made.

Mistletoe: Very popular in the 1970s.

Mothers: Often the butt of Christmas fun, so make sure you get yours a nice gift. Or, if you *are* the mother/butt, take it in good spirit or put a stop to it by announcing you have a serious *illness*.

Mulled wine: Very Christmassy, but better to call it *Glue Vine*.

Music: See *Slade* and *playlist*.

Myrrh: Good word for Christmas *poems*, but spell it correctly.

N

Napkins: Designer Christmas napkins can provide a talking point if conversation dries up ('Nice napkins', 'Orla Kiely', 'Oh'). And much needed in bookshop cafés.

Nativity: See *donkey*.

Needle drop: avoid needle drop by keeping the house as cold as possible.

NHS: God bless it and all who work in it – at Christmas and every day. See *time off work*.

Nigella: Lawson, very Christmassy.

Nut roast: Really quite nice, and comparatively moist. See *vegetarian*.

Nutcracker: (Tool) popular with attention-seekers who will crack nuts inexpertly, say how much they love walnuts, but only eat one. See *potpourri*.

Nutcracker: A two-act ballet by Tchaikovsky, popular with Cadbury's Fruit & Nut lovers.

O

'O Come, All Ye Faithful': Sam Frears' favourite carol.

Office party: See *works' do*.

One-at-a-Time Present Opening (OTPO): A tradition whereby presents are opened one person/present at a time while the assembly looks on. Tedious and embarrassing, on the whole, but good for *funny gifts*. See also *Christmas lovers* and *Vic*.

Onesie: Elderly relatives and *killjoys* sometimes tell youngsters they can't wear their reindeer onesie all day. Be prepared for this by greeting guests with the news that your youngster has had a wardrobe fire.

Oranges: All types of orange are Christmassy. Garnish for foods and drinks. Strew around to draw the eye from imperfection for Instagram. See *Terry's Chocolate Orange*.

P

Pantomime: Can be great fun, but decline tickets if it's a pantomime about a pantomime within a pantomime.

Parties: Serve *mince pies* and *Glue Vine* and try not to let anyone sit down. Hide your *Radio Times*.

Petrol station: Handy for last-minute gifts. See *shopping*.

Phone ban: Fine, ban phones – if you want to spend Christmas alone.

Phone calls: Christmas phone calls should be confined to people in prison or hospital (rules permitting) or to people who are, for some reason, all alone at Christmas.

Playlist: Share the burden by asking for help in compiling.

Poems: Send Christmas poems to your friend(s) instead of cards. See *U. A. Fanthorpe*.

Potpourri: Unnecessary. Christmas smells nice without.

Also, risk of people eating it due to snacky nature of Christmas. See *nutcracker.*

Harry Potter: Very Christmassy.

Precedent setting: Many opportunities at Christmas, none more so than the *advent calendar.*

Princess Anne: Very Christmassy and sensible at the same time. My favourite of the royals.

Pudding: The tradition of dousing a small shop-bought pudding with lighter fuel and setting fire to it is still popular. Make sure to switch off lights for full flame effect and know the whereabouts of your nearest exit and fire extinguisher. I serve *Delia*'s chocolate *yule log* for actually eating.

Purists: The 'three kings' were, in fact, an undisclosed number of wise men. Hear the purists out, uninterrupted, but ignore. See *donkey, Father Christmas* and *killjoys.*

Q

Quality Street: The only really Christmassy chocolates (except *Terry's Chocolate Orange*), more Christmassy than, say, *Heroes.*

Queen's Speech: A highlight for some, a nap opportunity for others – either way, a good thing. See *The King's Speech.*

R

Radio Times: The only part of Christmas that is

essential *and* traditional. Devise elaborate marking-up system using *highlighter pens.*

Refuse collectors: Memorize Christmas collection times and give a large cash gift to ensure year-long loyalty and care.

Re-gifting: One of the most exciting aspects of Christmas (risky but rewarding).

Robin redbreast: Christmassy and real. Team up with *holly* for red-and-green colour scheme.

Roses: Cadbury. Better than *Heroes* but not as good as *Quality Street.*

Round robin: Letter sent by people with high self-esteem at Christmas before Facebook was invented, sadly now endangered. Mocked by some but adored by me.

S

Santa Claus: American for *Father Christmas* (pronounced 'Sanna Clahs').

Santa*Land Diaries:* The story of Crumpet the Elf by David Sedaris. The funniest Christmas story.

Ebenezer Scrooge: A character in *A Christmas Carol* and a name for un-Christmassy people who keep saying they wish they were spending Christmas in the Alps.

Secret Santa: Do not take lightly. Your chance to shine in the workplace, school, college, home. See *Barbara Windsor.*

Shopping: I start my Christmas Shopping on 15th September. Vic starts straight after Diwali. Stella does hers on Christmas Eve.

'Silent Night': Unbearable.

Slade: 'Merry Xmas Everybody' must be on your Christmas *playlist*. Also, respect for spelling of *Xmas* (respect also to John and Yoko).

Snobbishness: The most un-Christmassy thing in the world, except for stealing a *wreath* from someone's front door.

Snow: Hand-drawn snowflakes on the window are the modern-day equivalent of the great fake windowsill snowdrifts of my day. Either is nice, unless you get the real thing.

Snowball: A disgusting drink made from a sickly beverage. See *eggnog*.

The Snowman: Is snuck on to televisual schedule every year by *Granny Kate*. See *Raymond Briggs, handkerchief.*

Stocking: Best is a bespoke stocking-shaped sack – never a pillowcase or bin liner, not Christmassy.

Stuffing: Jokes about stuffing never get old. See *Delia.*

T

Television: Viewing must be meticulously planned in advance using the *Radio Times*.

Terry's Chocolate Orange: Easy to wrap, available in 99p-land and very Christmassy.

Thanksgiving: For American people who can't wait for Christmas.

Time off work: the real *true meaning* of Christmas. See also *NHS*.

Tinsel: Jolly for decorating dog leads for Christmas walks and hiding bald patches on Christmas tree. Otherwise, not actually that nice, but see *snobbishness.*

Alan Titchmarsh: Very Christmassy and bears an uncanny resemblance to the Angel Gabriel.

Toyshop: Very Christmassy, good for seasonal work opportunities. See *elf costume.*

Tree: Preferably real, unless there's been an emergency (see *needle drop*). But fake ones are legit, and one should never indulge in *snobbishness.*

True meaning: Don't dwell on this too much. See *Jesus, time off work.*

Turkey: There are various ways of cooking to avoid *dryness.* But, sadly, unless you deep-fry or only eat the purple meat, it will remain dry. Naturally rich in *L-tryptophan.*

Twelfth Night: Either 5th or 6th January. Time to take down the Christmas *tree* and try out your new *Hoover.* Leaving decorations up past this date (whichever it is) could lead to bankruptcy in the coming year.

U

Underwear: Christmassy underwear can make a fun gift, but approach with caution. Avoid anything depicting turkeys or baubles, or stick to socks.

V

Vegetarian: Pretending to be vegetarian is a tactful way of avoiding turkey and Christmas pudding. See *nut roast*.

Vic: My sister and the most Christmassy person on earth, but can lash out if things don't go to plan. See *One-at-a-Time Present Opening (OTPO)*, *Christmas lovers*.

Vouchers: Boring, lazy, insulting, unless a personal pledge to wash the car (inside and out) and rinse sponge, or a marriage/sex proposal.

W

Walk: Yes, do get everyone out on a walk but don't force them all to link arms.

West London: Very Christmassy, good for *wreath* spotting. As are south Leicestershire, the Cotswolds and Edinburgh.

Barbara Windsor: *The Laughter and Tears of a Cockney Sparrow* – my greatest ever gift triumph. See *Secret Santa*.

Wishbone: The tradition of breaking a turkey

wishbone for luck was started either by the Romans
or the Pilgrims. See *fights*.

Works' do: Usually in November or January. Always
attend if you can. Don't get drunk and reminisce
about being blackballed by the village Brownie pack.
See *parties*.

Wrapping: Make an effort. Wrap with nice paper and
tie with ribbon. Get the shop to do it, if possible. See
Amazon.

Wreath: Do not steal the Christmas wreath from
someone's front door, no matter how posh the house.
It's possibly the most un-Christmassy thing you can
do – barring doing all your shopping on *Amazon*.
(West London is your best bet for wreath theft,
apparently.)

X

Xmas: No such word. My phone autocorrects 'Xmas' to
'Xanadu' without even asking me. But nothing wrong
with this abbreviation, it comes from the Greek (X
meaning 'Christ'). See also *Slade*.

Xmassy: Don't aim for a perfect Xmas, aim for an
Xmassy Xmas.

Y

Yule: Good word for Christmas *poems*, but spell it
correctly.

Yule log: A chocolate Swiss roll disguised as a log. Very popular with people who hate Christmas *pudding*.

Z

Zest: a vital ingredient in many Christmas dishes. Buy plenty of oranges and lemons and locate your zesting tool.

ACKNOWLEDGMENTS

Many thanks, as always, to colleagues at Penguin Books:

To my editor, Mary Mount, who claims to have come up with the idea for this book, and to Isabel Wall, who actually did. Also to Chantal Noel, Poppy North, Keith Taylor, Sarah Scarlett and Shân Morley Jones.

To my agent, Jo Unwin. And, finally, to booksellers across the land, especially my local – Waterstones, Truro.

I'm more thrilled than I can say that Reagan Arthur at Little, Brown has taken me on again. And I'd like to thank colleagues Joseph Lee, Katharine Myers, Jennifer Shaffer, Ira Boudah, Jayne Yaffe Kemp, and Julianna Lee.

ABOUT THE AUTHOR

Nina Stibbe was born in Leicester, England. She is the author of *Love, Nina*, which was shortlisted for the Waterstones Book of the Year Award and won a Non-Fiction Book of the Year Award at Britain's 2014 National Book Awards, and the highly acclaimed novels *Man at the Helm* and *Paradise Lodge,* which were both shortlisted for the Bollinger Everyman Wodehouse Prize for Comic Fiction. She lives in Cornwall.